scuba diver's guide to underwater ventures

Judy Gail May

Stackpole Books

SCUBA DIVER'S GUIDE TO UNDERWATER VENTURES

Copyright © 1973 by
THE STACKPOLE COMPANY

Published by
STACKPOLE BOOKS
Cameron and Kelker Streets
Harrisburg, Pa. 17105

Printed in the U.S.A.

Library of Congress Cataloging in Publication Data

May, Judy Gail.
  Scuba diver's guide to underwater ventures.

  1. Skin diving. I. Title.
GV840.S78M39 1973   797.2'3   73-9949
ISBN 0-8117-1513-2
ISBN 0-8117-2017-9 (pbk.)

TO DEAN

my diving buddy, technical advisor, unofficial editor, severest critic, greatest fan, and loving husband, without whom this book would never have been.

Contents

Acknowledgments   11

Preface   13

1 Entering the World of Diving   15

Physical Requirements   Basic Equipment   SCUBA Gear
Accessories   Rules and Regulations   A New Environment
Squeeze   Air Embolism   The Bends   Nitrogen Narcosis
Carbon Monoxide Poisoning   Entrance into the Underwater
World

2 Photographing the Underwater World   36

Learning Underwater Photography   A Different Environment
Cameras and Housings   Lenses   Film   Light Meters
Filters   Flash   Other Accessories   Maintenance and
Handling   Natural Light Techniques   Flash Techniques
Movie Photography and Equipment   Movie-Making Techniques

3 Diving for Treasure   66

Where to Look   Locating the Wreck   Setting Up and
Surveying the Site   Breathing Apparatus   Excavation
Lifting   Identifying the Wreck   Preservation of Artifacts
Laws Governing "Finds"   Weekend Treasure Hunters
Reporting the Find

4 Diving Beneath the Ice   91

Who Should Ice Dive?   Where to Dive   Keeping Warm
Planning the Dive   At the Site   The Life Line
Other Gear and Preparations   Under the Ice   Emergency

5 Fish-Watching in Fresh Water   106

Fish Identification   The Crustaceans   Mollusks
Amphibians   Reptiles   Locating and Attracting Freshwater
Life

6 Sightseeing in the Ocean   120

The Sea's Camouflage   Habits of Marine Animals
Dangerous Marine Animals   How to get to the Sea
Lobstering

7 Bring 'Em Back Alive   137

Open Water Vs. Pet Shop Fish   Where to Collect
Catching the Fish   Collecting Other Saltwater Creatures   Collecting
Freshwater Plants and Animals   Transporting the Catch
Setting Up the Aquarium   Decorating the Freshwater Tank
Decorating the Marine Tank   Water   Introducing Species
to the Tank   Feeding   Tank Care and
Maintenance

8   Shell Collecting on the Bottom   156

Why Dive for Shells?   What is a Shell?   Where to Dive
for Shells   Finding the Shells   Equipment   Dangerous
Shells   Cleaning and Preserving   Displaying the Shells

9   Coral Gathering   170

What is Coral?   Where to Find Coral   Stoney Coral
Identification   Collecting Coral   Cleaning and
Preserving the Specimen   Cleaning and Coral
Identification   Displaying the Coral

10   Cave Diving—Underwater Underground   186

How Caves Are Formed   Pioneers of Cave Diving
The Dangers of Cave Diving   Training for Cave
Diving   Equipment   Planning the Dive   In the Cave
Decompression   Debriefing   Where to Cave Dive

11   Careers in Diving   206

Passing on the Knowledge   Charter Captains   Dive Shop
Owner   Join the Navy and See the Underwater World
Diving Scientists   The Technician   Salvage, Construction
and Repair   "Test Pilot"   Photography   Resources
from the Sea   SCUBA Sheriffs and Diving Detectives
Other Occupations

Acknowledgments

I WOULD LIKE to extend my sincere thanks for their help and cooperation to Nikon Inc., subsidiary of Ehrenreich Photo-Optical Industries, Inc; Zodiac of North America; Evinrude Motors; ITT Decca Marine; Fiberbuilt Photo Products; Aqua Craft; Pan American Airlines; and the Bermuda Tourist Bureau. Also to LCDR Timothy Mennuti of the U.S. Navy and Jim Storey, cave diving specialist of the National Speleological Society (NSS). For their assistance in the archeology material, I would especially like to thank Commander Mendel Peterson, Director of Underwater Projects for the Smithsonian Institute; Teddy Tucker; and Educational Expeditions International.

Finally, I want to very personally thank all the members of the Metuchen Underwater Divers Club for their assistance and enthusiasm; Al Catalfumo of the Diver's Cove; and last, but not least, Joe Strykowski, who started it all.

(Photos by the author unless otherwise indicated.)

Preface

THOUSANDS OF PEOPLE learn to scuba dive every year and, each succeeding year, that number keeps growing.

Within a year after their graduation, however, over 50% of these new divers, who were so eager to enter the underwater world, stop diving. Why? Because once the newness wears off, they don't know what to do with themselves underwater.

The problem is that no one tells them about the wonderful, exciting underwater activities that are within their reach, now that they know how to dive.

To help fill this need, I have developed this book as a first, basic introduction and guide to the numerous activities the scuba diver can enjoy. From its pages, I hope the novice divers—and those veterans looking for new fun underwater—will choose activities that most appeal to them and have many happy, safe hours underwater.

Finally, I'd like to note that for the sake of simplicity, I have referred to "the diver" as "he". This certainly does not mean that diving is only a man's sport. As a female diver myself, I can assure every girl reading this book that she can enjoy the underwater world, too.

Judy Gail May

1 Entering the World of Diving

LESS THAN 30 years ago, the underwater world was a vast, forbidding secret domain where only a few professional divers and marine scientists might venture. They were tied to the surface by the umbilical cord of an air line, and further limited by weighted shoes and the heavy, cumbersome diving dress.

Then in 1943, the first practical SCUBA equipment was tested and marketed in France, and the door to the underwater world was unlocked. Behind that door was discovered submerged mountains, valleys and vast sandy plains to be explored. And the myriads of brightly colored sea creatures accepted this bubbling man-fish as just another predator to be approached with caution.

SCUBA stands for self-contained underwater breathing apparatus. As the phrase implies, the diver carries all his

15

needed air with him. He has no tie to the surface, which leaves him as free and as mobile as a fish.

In the early days of diving, the pioneers of the sport were enthralled with the sheer novelty of being able to breathe underwater and see sights never witnessed by man. But as this novelty wore off, they began using their time underwater for practical activities. They moved into the spheres of underwater construction and exploration, making notable contributions to archeology, marine biology, geology and industry.

Today's novice sport diver goes through a similar transition. On his first few dives he is thoroughly occupied with his new environment, testing his weightlessness, listening to the whistle of his breathing, and gazing in awe at the unbelievable sights around him. However, when the newness has passed, he begins looking for something to do—for some activity to give purpose and direction to his diving.

Opportunities for underwater activities abound in this new and versatile sport. The photography buff will find a studio setup behind every coral head, the adventurer will discover the excitement of diving in caves and under the ice, the naturalist will revel in the wondrous fish life to be observed and studied. There is an underwater hobby for each and every diver.

Before pursuing any of these exciting activities underwater, the enthusiast must fulfill one important prerequisite—he must first be a diver. Thanks to the development of safer, simpler, and more popularly priced equipment, SCUBA diving has become a sport that is accessible to nearly everyone. But this does not mean that one can become a diver by merely strapping a tank on his back and entering the water.

No one in his right mind would go to an army surplus store, buy a parachute, and then—without instruction or professional guidance—make a parachute jump of 10,000 feet. It is equally important to get *certified* instruction before attempting to dive. A great many diving accidents have occurred because the diver was taught in "one-easy lesson" by a friend who had learned the same way.

The YMCA was the first national organization to offer certified scuba instruction. Theirs is one of the most comprehensive courses offered, and can be found at well over 50% of the YMCAs and YWCAs in the country. Another excellent source of training is the National Association of Underwater Instructors (NAUI), an organization devoted entirely to certifying instructors, setting up guidelines for courses, and certifying students who pass their courses. NAUI instructors teach at local pools for the most part, and information about their courses can often be obtained at the local dive shop. Other nationally recognized certifying bodies are the Professional Association of Diving Instructors (PADI) and L. A. County. Any one of these associations offers a safe entry into the sport of scuba diving.

A secondary reason for obtaining certified instruction, is that the graduating student is issued a "C" card. In more and more dive shops, owners will not sell or rent equipment nor fill tanks unless the diver can show a recognized "C" card.

PHYSICAL REQUIREMENTS

The prospective diver does not need to be an Olympic swimmer. Nor can he be a non-swimmer. Although swimming skills are not actually needed while diving, the non-swimmer will be self-conscious and wary in the water, where the swimmer will feel at home. More importantly, in case his equipment is lost or must be ditched, the swimmer will have a way to get to the safety of the shore or his boat.

A diver must be in good health. Anyone with a bad heart, respiratory ailments, epilepsy, chronic sinusitis or any other disabling condition should not dive. In fact, almost every scuba instructor requires the applicant to pass a medical examination before enrollment in his course.

BASIC EQUIPMENT

Three basic pieces of equipment are the mask, snorkle and fins. Diving with this fundamental equipment is called snorkling. Snorkling can be a lot of fun in itself, and, particularly in warm tropical waters, the scuba diver may spend two hours a day scuba diving but four or five more snorkling on the shallow reefs.

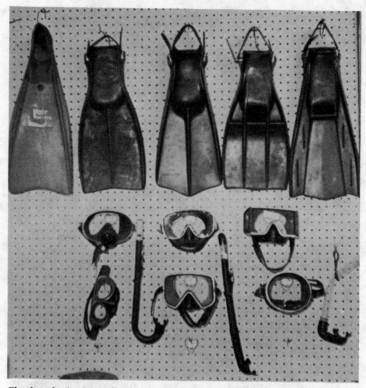

The three basic pieces of equipment are mask, fins and snorkle. Pictured above are several varieties of each. In the upper left corner is a full foot pocket fin. The other four are open heel types with stiffer blades. The snorkle at left is the ordinary "J" type, the center one has a flexible curve, and the one at the right is the big-barrel snorkle.

The new diver should thoroughly master the use of these three pieces of equipment before going on to scuba gear, because the same swimming techniques he learns will continue to be used when he adds his breathing apparatus.

The *mask* is the window to the underwater world. It provides an air space between the diver's eyes and the water, allowing him to see as clearly as if he was on land.

A mask for diving must fit well. The rubber skirt of the mask should be flexible enough to mold itself to the contours of the face and form a tight seal. If the mask does not seal, it will continue to leak throughout the dive. A test for proper fit is to place the mask on the face without putting the band on and inhale through the nose. If the mask stays on the face without being held, it fits properly. If it falls off, it is too large or shaped wrong.

The glass must be shatterproof but never plastic and should be held in place by an adjustable metal band. For those who wear glasses, optically ground lenses are available for most masks.

If the mask should become flooded underwater, the diver does not need to surface. All he must do is gently press the upper edge of the mask—the one closest to the surface—and exhale through his nose into the mask in short puffs. His air will displace the water and empty the mask. Mask clearing is an important procedure to learn because a diver without a mask is virtually blind underwater.

The lens of the mask will often fog when diving, because of the difference in temperature between the air inside and the water outside. Although there are a number of products on the market for defogging the lens, the simplest method is to rub a little saliva on the inside of the faceplate and rinse it off. This will usually keep the lens clear for the duration of the dive.

The snorkle is simply a hollow breathing tube, made of hard rubber or plastic, approximately 12 to 15 inches long. There are several different shapes, the most common being the "J"-shaped snorkle. Attached to the tube is a soft rubber mouthpiece which fits under the lips and is held gently between the teeth. The tube of the snorkle is usually slipped under the mask strap and rests against the side of the face.

A snorkle allows the skin diver to swim on the surface without lifting his head to take a breath, thereby conserving as much as 30% of his energy. It enables him to swim long distances and stay in the water for hours without getting tired. For the scuba diver, the snorkle is a vital piece of safety equipment. Surfacing with an empty tank and facing a long swim to his boat or the shore, he would find the swim an ordeal without a snorkle.

If water fills the snorkle due to the wave action or the diver going beneath the surface, it can be removed by simply exhaling sharply before taking the first breath.

Fins, or flippers as they are also called, give the diver the ability to go faster and farther while using much less energy than he would without them. Also, since the arm stroke is not necessary when using fins, they free his hands for carrying a camera or "treasures" that he brings up from the bottom.

There are two basic types of fins—full foot pocket and open heel fins. Choosing between the two types is purely a matter of personal preference. The full foot pocket fins are usually sold by shoe size. The open heel fins come in small, medium and large and should be worn over a neoprene boot. In each case it is important to get a good fit.

The stiffness in the blade varies. The stiffer the blade, the more power and thrust the fin gives, but a very rigid blade may be too much for the leg muscles of a neophyte diver. On the other hand, a very, very soft blade will make the diver work too hard, because he will have to take more strokes to get through the water.

The fins exert their propelling force only when they move through the water parallel to the surface. For this reason, the knees must be kept straight and the toes pointed when swimming with fins.

The basic kick is called the flutter kick and comes from the hips. It is slow and rhythmic. The fins should never be lifted out of the water on the upward stroke. Raising the head slightly will lower the feet and keep the fins underwater.

Once the diver is thoroughly familiar with the snorkling gear, he is ready to begin working with the breathing apparatus. Initially, he should practice with the equipment in a swimming pool.

SCUBA GEAR

The sport diver's underwater breathing apparatus is made up of three primary parts: the tank, the valve, and the regulator. It is called an open circuit system because the diver exhales into the water, rather than reusing the air. With this system he breathes compressed *air*—not pure oxygen as so many people erroneously believe.

The *tank* is a one-piece seamless cylinder for holding high pressure air. Most tanks are made of high-quality chrome-molybdenum steel, although a new aluminum tank is now on the market. The volume of a tank is expressed in the cubic feet of compressed air that the tank holds when filled to maximum pressure. Maximum tank pressure is usually 2250 pounds per square inch (psi) and the volume of the average-sized tank is 71.2 cubic feet.

When more air is needed for long or deep dives, the 71.2 cubic foot tanks can be hooked together as doubles or even triples. There are 50 cubic foot tanks available for children

These tanks display various types of rigs. The standing tanks at left are a set of doubles connected by a double yoke. To the right of these is a tank with a "K" (nonreserve) valve with an emergency pony bottle attached. The tank at right has a "J" valve in the "on" position.

Note in the upper right-hand corner, the black tank has a cap. When tanks are stored without valves, they must be capped or moisture may enter the tank.

Remembering that a tank is a potential bomb and must not be allowed to roll around the deck, these divers have constructed a rack for stacking the tanks.

and women, in addition to a 90 cubic foot unit for extra capacity in a single tank.

The law requires that all tanks be hydrostatically tested and certified by the Department of Transportation every 5 years. The tank is stamped with the date of last certification when it passes, or destroyed if it fails. Because of the great amount of use a scuba tank usually gets, it is recommended that the tank be sent in for testing every three years and be taken to a dive shop and given a visual check for interior corrosion every year.

Since the filled tank is highly pressurized, it is a potential bomb. If the air in a full tank was suddenly released, it could drive the tank through a brick wall. It must therefore be handled with care and never dropped or banged. Since heat will make the air expand, it must never be left in the sun or stored in a hot place.

The *valve* regulates the flow of air to and from the tank. It is screwed, finger-tight, into a threaded opening in the top of the tank. There are two types of valves on the market today—K valves and J valves. The K valve is a non-reserve valve which operates like a water faucet, simply turning the air on or off. When it is on, the diver has access to all the air in the tank and can breathe it dry.

The J valve is a spring-loaded valve that has the added safety feature of having a calibrated spring mechanism which holds 300 psi of air in reserve. When the air in the tank drops to 300 psi, this spring shuts off the air as a warning to the diver that he is getting near to the end of his supply. He can then manually pull his reserve rod which releases the remaining air.

The *regulator* is the heart of the SCUBA system. Its important function is to feed the air to the diver at a breathable pressure equal to that of the surrounding water. It operates on a "demand" principle, automatically delivering air as the diver inhales, and then cutting off the flow of air as he exhales.

There are many types of regulators on the market and selection is mainly a matter of personal preference. The most popular type today is the single-hose, two-stage regulator. The two-stage reduces the high pressure air in the tank to breathable pressure in two steps instead of one, making it much easier for the diver to draw a breath.

A submersible pressure gauge may be attached to the high pressure port on the regulator for convenience and as

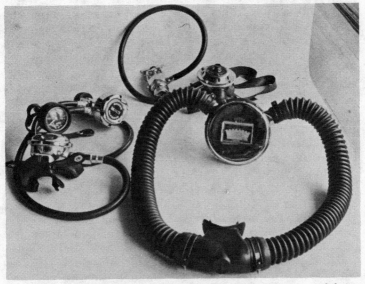

The type of regulator a diver uses is a matter of personal preference. At left, is a single-stage regulator with a submersible pressure gauge attached. In the rear is another model of a single hose regulator without the pressure gauge, but with a neck strap attached. At right is an older model double-hose regulator.

an added safety measure. This gauge gives the reading of the tank pressure, so that the diver knows, at a glance, how much air he has left in his tank and can plan his dive accordingly.

When the tank, valve and regulator are assembled, they are held on the diver's back by means of a harness. The harness consists of a back pack and shoulder and waist straps. All straps must be equipped with quick release buckles or snaps so that they can be opened quickly and easily if the diver needs to ditch his equipment in an emergency situation underwater.

In cold water below 70 degrees, an exposure suit must be worn to minimize loss of body heat. Heat is conducted from the body 25 times faster in water than in air. For this reason a temperature that would be comfortable on land might be unbearable for any length of time underwater.

For the sport diver, the most popular type of exposure suit is the *wet suit*. It is made of foam neoprene, which is a rubbery material containing thousands of tiny bubbles. It is called a wet suit because it traps a thin layer of water between the diver's skin and the suit. This small volume of water is warmed quickly to body temperature and the insulation of the neoprene keeps the cold of the surrounding water from drawing off body heat and chilling the diver. Suits and accessories—which include boots, gloves, hoods and vests—may be purchased in thicknesses ranging from 1/8 inch to 3/8 inch depending on the temperature of the water the diver will be swimming in.

A new development in exposure suits is the Unisuit, which combines the best features of both wet and dry suits. It is airtight and keeps the diver dry. For the diver who does much very cold water diving, it is ideal. In addition, it has the advantage of allowing the diver to control his buoyancy by inflating and deflating his suit.

Since the equipped diver will now be quite buoyant, he must wear lead weights around his waist to offset this buoyancy and enable him to get below the surface. These weights are strung on a strong nylon belt which must be equipped with a quick release buckle. It should be the last piece of equipment donned so that it can be jettisoned first if the need arises.

A diver floats lazily on the surface, buoyed up by the inflatable dry wet suit, the Unisuit. In addition to keeping the diver warm and dry, it can be used to control his buoyancy and to serve as an emergency float at the surface.

ACCESSORIES

In addition to this essential scuba equipment, there are several important accessories that the safe diver should have. A *depth gauge* should be worn on the wrist. This instrument registers the diver's depth in feet beneath the surface. It is an important gauge because depth is nearly impossible to estimate. Clear water is deceptive. The diver may be able to see the bottom although it is 150 feet below. In murky water, where the diver can see neither the surface nor the bottom, he has no way of even estimating his depth without a gauge.

The newest innovation in depth gauges is the digital depth gauge. It is transistorized and begins operating the minute it is put into the water. It gives a reading in one foot increments.

Another vital wrist accessory is the *diving watch*. Not every waterproof watch is a diving watch. It must be waterproof and designed to withstand the pressure. The maximum depth to which the watch is guaranteed is usually stamped or printed on the watch. This may be expressed in feet (pressure resistant to 300 feet) or in atmospheres (guaranteed to 10 atmospheres). Approximately 33 feet equal one atmosphere.

An essential piece of safety equipment is an *inflatable life vest*. It can keep a fully-equiped diver afloat and may save his life. The vest can be inflated orally or by means of a CO2 cartridge. It should not be inflated on the bottom to bring a diver to the surface. This would result in a very rapid uncontrolled ascent which could be dangerous and even fatal.

A handy tool is the *diver's knife*. It is not a weapon for fending off sharks, but can be extremely helpful to the diver who becomes entangled in lines, kelp or nets. It is normally worn in a sheath, strapped to the leg.

To assure that equipment is in working condition at all times, proper maintenance is essential. Salt water and chlorine are both very harmful to the rubber and metal parts of the gear. After diving in the ocean or in a pool, the diver should rinse all gear thoroughly in fresh water before storage.

There are many other accessories, tools and pieces of equipment that the diver might use. Most of these relate to a specific activity underwater and will be discussed in the related chapter.

Equipment should be purchased from a reputable dive shop or divers' supply company, rather than the sporting goods counter of the neighborhood discount store. The quality of gear carried in the discount store is often low, plus there usually is no one there qualified to give the new diver expert advice while he is making his first purchases.

RULES AND REGULATIONS

The first and most important rule of diving is NEVER DIVE ALONE. Divers must always follow "the buddy system", entering and leaving the water in pairs. This means no matter how many divers are in the group, each diver has one buddy, whom he must keep in sight at all times.

If the water is exceptionally murky or dark, a buddy line should be used. This is a short line tied to the wrist of each of the divers so that they cannot inadvertently wander away from each other.

If a diver is ever separated from his buddy, the best procedure to follow is to surface. Then, if his partner does not appear on the surface in a matter of minutes, he can begin emergency procedures.

A second rule to remember is STOP AND THINK. More diving accidents occur because the diver panicked than for any other reason. In an unusual or frightening situation, if the diver takes a moment to pause and think rationally before acting, he is less likely to do an impulsive and dangerous deed.

Thirdly, a diver should NEVER DIVE WHEN he is NOT FEELING FIT. Diving is an energetic sport, and a diver who is below par from an illness or lack of rest may not have the strength needed to bring himself safely back from the dive. Divers also should exercise during the off seasons to keep in good physical condition, and start slowly by working out in a pool or in shallow water at the beginning of each new season.

A NEW ENVIRONMENT

When the diver dons his gear and enters the underwater world, he is going into a strange and foreign environment.

Following the buddy system, a pair of divers prepare to enter the water together from the stern of a dive boat. The diver at left wears a conventional wet suit, while the other has on the new Unisuit, especially made for cold water like the 40 degree Atlantic behind them.

Many things are different here. As he descends, the world around him loses color, becoming more and more blue. He feels weightless and can move effortlessly in any direction.

He feels like a superman because he can lift heavy objects that would be immovable on land. Yet, his own movements are slow, restricted by the drag of the water which is hundreds of times more dense than the air.

Speech is impossible in this environment. To communicate he must use hand signals, or make noises such as rapping on his tank with a knife to get his buddy's attention. His hearing seems impaired. Sound travels five times faster in water than in air, and because of its increased speed, it is nearly impossible to determine where a particular sound is coming from.

The new diver feels truly out of his element, because the physical rules that he lived by on land are invalid here. The more he visits this world, however, the more used to these phonomenon he will become, until finally he is as at home underwater as he is on land.

No matter how familiar the diver becomes with the underwater world, this doesn't change the fact that it is a different environment. The diver must be aware of these differences in order to understand and avoid diving problems. The most serious of these problems are squeeze, embolisms, the bends and nitrogen narcosis.

SQUEEZE

The human body is, for the most part, pressure resistant. On land, every day, each person had nearly 15 pounds of pressure on every square inch of his body. This is because air has weight. The measurement of this weight is made from the outer limits of the atmosphere to the earth at sea level, and is expressed as one atmosphere of pressure.

Water weighs far more than air. To add one atmosphere of water pressure to the air pressure already on him, the diver descends only 33 feet. Every 33 feet of descent adds another atmosphere of pressure.

The solids and liquids in the body are not affected by this increasing pressure—but the air spaces are. As the diver descends, the air that is trapped in his lungs, his middle ear, his sinus cavitites and his intestines is compressed and decreased in volume. If the air in these spaces is not equalized with the higher water pressure, the diver experiences a problem called Squeeze.

The ear is one of the first places the diver will experience Squeeze. As he descends, he may feel a slight pain or fullness in his ears. This occurs because air trapped in the middle ear is decreasing in volume and the water pressure is pressing on the eardrum to attempt to equalize this pressure.

This is easy to remedy. The best method is to close off the nostrils and exhale sharply through the nose. Most masks have finger wells or rubber nose pieces to make clearing the ears easy.

This method of clearing equalizes the pressure by forcing air through the Eustachian tube into the middle ear chamber. The Eustachian tube goes from the back of the throat to the middle ear.

Some people can clear their ears by yawning, swallowing or wiggling their jaw from side to side. This stretches the Eustachian tube and opens it so that air can pass through. However, if the diver has a cold or allergy which swells the tube, no amount of clearing will equalize the ears; the diver should not attempt to dive, or he will risk a ruptured eardrum. A descent of less than 10 feet could rupture an eardrum, so the diver must heed the warning pain.

The sinus cavities clear themselves with no help from the diver. But, they too can become swollen from head colds or sinusitis, which will cause a very sharp pain just over or under the eyes. Again, the diver must leave the water and not dive until the condition clears up.

Air spaces that the diver attaches to himself may also cause trouble. The diver puts a mask on at the surface and then descends into greater pressure. The pressure will push the mask against his face and cause a suction. This can be remedied by simply exhaling through the nose into the mask. For this reason, goggles which do not cover the nose cannot be worn by the scuba diver.

AIR EMBOLISM

Since the volume of air is decreased as the diver descends, it follows that it will increase as he comes up.

This presents no problem as long as the diver breathes normally. If, however, he takes a breath at the bottom and holds it as he ascends, the air in his lungs will expand.

The lungs are very delicate and this expansion could cause them to burst. If the lungs rupture, air bubbles can be forced into the blood vessels where they will continue to expand and cause a blockage. The bubbles will often lodge in the vessels to the brain, cutting off the oxygen supply.

Air embolism is not only a deep water problem. A difference of only four feet of increased pressure could cause a fully inflated lung to rupture. To avoid air embolism, the

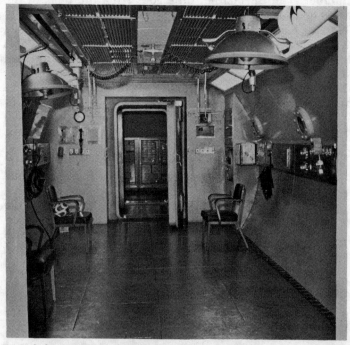

Pictured above is one of the large chambers of the St. Barnabas Medical Center recompression facility in Livingston, N.J. The facility, having two large chambers and two small chambers, is the largest in the world. This chamber is equipped as an operating room in addition to having recompression capabilities.

The chambers are controlled by a technician and monitored through closed circuit television.

diver must only remember to exhale as he is ascending. This problem most often happens to the panicked, novice diver who heads for the surface in a rush, instinctively holding his breath out of fear. Following the rule "Stop and Think" would avoid this danger.

If a diving buddy comes to the surface with a bloody froth at the mouth and/or loses consciousness, he must be rushed to a chamber for recompression. In the chamber, the pressure is increased to reduce the size of the bubbles and allow normal circulation to resume in the blood vessels. Then the diver is gradually brought back to surface pressure.

It should be part of the planning of every dive to know the location of the nearest operating decompression chamber. (A complete national list can be found in the University of Rhode Island booklet, "Scuba Safety Series, Report No. 3" which can be obtained by sending $1.00 to U. of R.I. Scuba Safety Project, 227 Wales Hall, U. of R.I., Kingston, RI 02881).

THE BENDS

Another divers' illness that must be treated in a recompression chamber is Decompression Sickness—more commonly known as The Bends. The condition was first recognized by the French scientist Paul Bert in the 1870s, when he observed helmet divers who would come up with intense pain in their joints and sometimes lose consciousness and even die.

The first medical notice of the disease was made during the digging of the pier excavations for the Brooklyn Bridge. The workers would come up from the dry pressurized shafts in twisted, bent body positions. From the sight of these men, the condition got the name, The Bends.

The Bends are caused by nitrogen under pressure at depth being forced into solution in the blood stream. The longer the diver is down and the deeper he goes, the more nitrogen goes into solution. Under normal conditions, as he ascends the nitrogen will come out of solution and be exhaled.

But, if he ascends too fast, the effect will be like uncapping a warm bottle of carbonated soda. While the bottle is capped and under pressure, the CO_2 is in solution. As soon as it is opened and the pressure decreased, the gas comes bubbling out. In the same way, nitrogen coming out of solution too quickly will form bubbles in the blood stream.

These will lodge in the areas of least circulation, particularly in the joints. In mild cases they will cause pain. In severe cases, the nitrogen bubbles can lodge in the spinal column, causing permanent paralysis or even death.

There are two ways for the sport diver to avoid the bends. One is to stay within the limits of the no-decompression table. This table give the maximum amount of bottom time for each depth.

Depth in Feet	Bottom Time in Minutes
33 (or less)	No time limit
35	310
40	200
50	100
60	60
70	50

80	40
90	30
100	25
110	20
120	15
130	10
140	10
150	5

When using this table, the deepest point reached on the dive must be used for computing the depth. Bottom time is the number of minutes from the moment the diver leaves the surface until he begins his ascent—not only the time spent on the bottom or at the deepest point of the dive.

The diver should also remember to come up slowly—at a rate of about 60 feet per minute or not faster than his smallest air bubbles are ascending.

If the diver wishes to go beyond the no-decompression limits, he must follow the U.S. Navy Decompression Tables and make stage decompression stops on the way up. These stops give the nitrogen time to come out of solution safely.

A diver suffering from The Bends must be rushed to the nearest recompression chamber for treatment. Time is of the essence. Someone should accompany him, if possible, who can give the chamber operater the necessary information such as how deep he was diving when the accident occurred.

NITROGEN NARCOSIS

Another effect of nitrogen under pressure is Nitrogen Narcosis, or Rapture of the Depths. In this condition, the nitrogen becomes an intoxicant and the diver may suddenly become confused and disoriented. The condition does not normally occur above 150 feet, but it varies with each diver and even with each dive. A diver may be affected today at 130 feet and tomorrow may feel fine at 170 feet.

Narcosis occurs in stages, and as the diver descends it

The diver gives the "OK" signal—an internationally recognized sign for telling his buddy that all is well, or for saying yes.

Note also that the diver wears a second emergency regulator around his neck.

becomes more and more acute. At first, the diver will feel light-hearted and gay, perhaps a bit silly. Next, his inhibitions are released and he may attempt dangerous acts that he would otherwise avoid. Often he loses his sense of direction at this point and can't tell up from down. The final stage is complete relaxation, in which the diver will often drop his mouthpiece and simply drown.

If his buddy has the presence of mind to drag him up to

shallower water, the symptoms will vanish as quickly as they came, with no aftereffects. This is one form of drunkenness without a hangover.

Inexperienced divers should stay above 150 feet and later learn their own tolerences. Even professional divers will ascend when they feel the effects of rapture of the depths creeping up on them.

CARBON-MONOXIDE POISONING

One additional danger to consider is carbon-monoxide poisoning. It can only occur if contaminated air is used in filling the air cylinders. If a gas-driven compressor is either not properly maintained or the intake port is improperly placed, exhaust fumes may get into the compressor's air intake. Breathing air with carbon-monoxide will cause dizziness and finally unconsciousness, and the deeper the diver goes the more toxic the gas becom the numerous diving clubs and organizations.

With a little experience under his weight belt, the diver is ready to make a choice from among the numerous underwater hobbies and activities that await him. For the trained diver, the hazards are minimal and the rewards are years of fun and excitment in the last frontier on earth.

2 Photographing the Underwater World

A SCUBA DIVER is one of the elite few who are privileged to visit the underwater world, view its beauty, and uncover its mysteries. But, after a dive, when he returns to his uninitiated friends, he finds it hard to describe his experiences to the non-divers. No spoken or written word can truly capture the beauty of a reef, the majesty of submarine mountains, or the frolicking of a pair of angelfish playing tag.

The old Chinese proverb that one picture is worth ten thousand words holds the key to the solution of this problem. Through the art of underwater photography, a diver can capture the submarine scene and carry it back to the surface with him. His photographs will enable him to share his scuba experience and will also serve him as a delightful reminder of past excursions beneath the water.

Photos offer the opportunity for unhurried observation, so the diver may even spot things in a photograph that his eyes missed during the dive. Photography can, in this way, enrich his diving experiences. This is particularly useful at great depths where, due to the effects of nitrogen, the diver's powers of observation are sharply decreased.

Underwater photography has many scientific and technical uses, too. It serves the marine biologist, the technician, the marine engineer, the navy man, and many, many others.

For the amateur diver, it's a great way to spend his time underwater—and it's just plain fun!

LEARNING UNDERWATER PHOTOGRAPHY

Underwater photography is not as formidable and complicated an activity as it may seem. Even a novice diver can enjoy it, and can produce original and imaginative shots. This is particularly true in the last few years during which inexpensive and simple-to-operate camera equipment has been developed, making the art of underwater photography accessible to the budgets and talents of most divers.

The diver who has no photographic experience at all should first read some books on photography in general and shoot several practice rolls of film on land. The new diver can be practicing above-water techniques with a camera while he is perfecting his diving skills to the point where he is ready to take on an underwater activity such as photography.

The clear, clean water of a swimming pool is a good practice ground for the new aquatic shutter-bug. There, he need not worry about currents, murky water or other open-water problems. He can concentrate on content and technique. He may use other divers or swimmers as models and, in the shallow water of a pool, he is able to surface often to direct and pose them.

A DIFFERENT ENVIRONMENT

The beginner will find conditions very different when he submerges his photography skills and experience. Most obviously, of course, he can't take his ordinary surface camera down and expect it to work. It will get wet and be ruined. So, either the camera must be protected from the destructive effects of water or a special submersible camera must be substituted.

Secondly, shooting through water is far different from shooting through air. Even the cleanest and clearest waters appear somewhat cloudy or foggy. One reason for this is that microscopic plankton (tiny animals and plants) are present in all water to a greater or lesser degree. Add to this the tiny bits of silt present, and the underwater photographer has quite a visibility problem to overcome. The particles in the water form a light-absorbing barrier between the camera and the subject. This barrier diminishes the available light, and also affects the ability of the diver to see. Visibility is a term used to express the number of feet a diver. can see laterally. To get good photos, the diver should divide this number by four. For example, if he can see up to 60 feet away, he should attempt to capture objects no more than 15 feet from his camera.

Light penetration is another factor to be considered in underwater photography. When light strikes the surface of the water, all of it does not penetrate. Some of it is

reflected and deflected back off the water. In a calm sea about 5 percent of the light bounces back, but when the surface is choppy, as much as 30 percent can be deflected.

The defusion of light also does some strange things to color. Beginning on the red end of the color spectrum, the warm colors disappear first. At 25 feet below the surface, red is almost completely absorbed. Orange is gone at 30 feet, followed by yellow and green. Blue is the only color left below 100 feet. Thus, without corrective measures, all underwater photographs would be a monochromatic blue. This can be corrected because the colors are actually present at depth, even though without artificial light neither the diver nor his camera can see them.

Due to refraction, the bending of light rays as they pass from the water into the air space of the camera, apparent size and distance are also affected. Subjects appear one-fourth larger and 25 percent closer then they actually are. This causes a normal lens to have a telephoto effect when used underwater. Refraction is not as great a problem as it may seem since the diver and the camera "see" alike underwater. The diver simply sets his distance as he sees it and not as he knows it really is, because the camera too, will record the apparent—not actual—distance.

To solve all the particular problems of underwater photography, special equipment has been designed. In addition, pioneer underwater photographers have developed specific corrective techniques which they have passed on to the diving community at large.

CAMERAS AND HOUSINGS

Early scuba divers dropped their surface cameras into makeshift housings like plastic bags, rubber gloves, hot water bottles, and other contrivances to keep the cameras dry underwater. The diving industry has come a long way since then. Today, equipment is available to fit individual needs and prices range from $50.00 for a complete outfit to thousands of dollars for professional-quality equipment.

For the very beginner, the ideal unit is a snapshot camera, like the Instamatic, in an inexpensive plexiglas housing. Most snapshot cameras have fixed focus, fixed

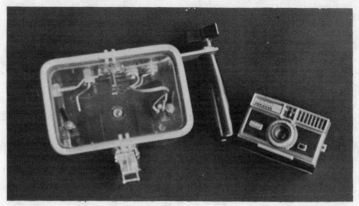

A simple snapshot camera can be slipped into the plexiglas housing, pictured above, making an excellent, inexpensive unit for the beginner.

shutter speed, and automatic electric eyes, so the photographer need adjust no controls—all he has to do is aim and shoot. Another advantage of these cameras is that they take 126 instant-loading film cartridges and so are easy to load and unload between dives.

The only variable the photographer must be concerned with, when using a snapshot camera, is the speed of the film he uses. The simplicity of the camera is somewhat limiting as it is difficult to get good pictures in bad light or poor visibility. However, for the beginner who wants to learn composition and use of a camera underwater without worrying about all the complicated settings, it is ideal.

For the serious amateur, and even for the professional underwater photographer, the best and most flexible underwater camera is the Nikonos, designed especially for the scuba diver, and now manufactured by Nikon, Inc. The Nikonos is an amphibious 35mm camera that requires no additional housing. The camera's own housing, made of corrosion-resistant metal covered with black vinyl, is pressure resistant and waterproof. Its parts are all O-ring sealed.

The camera is small and compact—about half the size of the smallest underwater housing for a 35mm camera. It is pressure tested to 160 feet and has simplified, oversized

Pictured at top is the Nikonos II, the submersible 35mm camera. The underwater sportsfinder is attached. At bottom is the disassembled camera. Its simple 3-piece construction makes it quick and easy to load and unload.

The diver wears a Nikonos camera on a neck strap. Note the smallness and compactness of this submersible camera that needs no housing.

controls for easy handling underwater—even with wet suit gloves. It is also excellent as a rugged, all-weather surface camera. Most of the photos in this book—both underwater and above—were taken with a Nikonos II camera. (The II indicates the model most current at this writing.)

The one drawback of the Nikonos is that it is not a reflex viewing camera. Distances must be estimated, rather than the focus set with through-the-lens viewing.

The Nikonos is moderately priced at around $200. This is

particularly economical considering that no additional money need be spent on a housing. There are, however, so many lenses and accessories available for this basic camera that the avid underwater photographer could amass over $2,000 worth of specialized equipment to go with his camera if he wishes.

If the diver wants to invest in a more expensive reflex viewing camera, or already has a good surface camera he wishes to use, there are housings available for most popular 35mm cameras. The housings are made of metal (usually cast aluminum) and Plexiglas or Lucite. Metal housings are expensive but offer greater strength and durability. Since they can be moulded to the shape of the camera they are usually less bulky. Plexiglas housings are considerably less expensive and, since they are transparent, have the advantage of allowing the diver to view his camera parts. The material welds into sturdy joints, but the housings are bulky and scratch easily.

The ideal housing should be neutrally or slightly negative buoyant for easy handling. Other features to look for are ease in reloading, simple controls, and a good framing or sighting device.

Some divers have made their own plexiglas housings out of 3/8 inch clear plastic. The control levers can be purchased from several of the diving supply companies. Whether a housing is bought or home-made, the diver should take it down empty on a test dive before putting a valuable camera in it. If no water is found inside, the housing is safe to use.

LENSES

Standard camera lens can be categorized as wide-angle, normal and telephoto. The wide-angle lens covers a wider area and allows the photographer to get closer to a large subject. The telephoto lens covers a narrower area but subjects can be captured from farther away.

For most underwater photography, the wide-angle lens is best. Since it allows the diver to get closer to his subject, there will be less water and fewer particles between the camera and the subject, resulting in a clearer picture. A wide-angle lens also provides greater depth of field. This means that when a point of focus is set, more of the immediate background and foreground will also be in focus. Unless optically corrected, however, a wide-angle lens will take a picture underwater which is not clear on the edges.

The Nikonos has a 28mm lens designed especially for underwater use. It is optically corrected to provide full compensation for distortion. The 28mm lens takes in about the same angle as a 35mm does on the surface. The 35mm, which is standard with the Nikonos camera, is also a good underwater lens, giving a slightly telephoto effect underwater. In addition, several companies make 21mm lenses for the Nikonos which are optically corrected for underwater use. On the opposite end of the spectrum, for shooting wary creatures who cannot be approached closely, an 80mm lens is available.

There are many tiny creatures of the underwater world—coral polyps, minute shells, damselfish—that can only be captured in a close-up picture. This requires a very short subject-to-camera distance. With standard lenses, most cameras cannot focus closer than two or three feet, so supplemental close-up lenses or extension tubes are needed.

A close-up lens, normally attached in front of the camera lens, shortens the focal length of the camera lens to which it is attached. Extension tubes have no lenses in them and fit between the camera body and the lens, extending the lens-to-film distance, thus creating a larger projected image.

One of the newest and most effective underwater close-up systems are the Green Things Macro Lenses called Un-Tension Tubes. Distributed by Aqua-Craft, Inc. of San Diego, these lenses are made for the Nikonos and combine the magnification ability of extension tubes and the versatility of close-up lenses. Their handiest feature is that they can be installed and removed underwater. Thus, the diver does not have to surface to change lenses when he finds a subject for macrophotography.

Un-Tension Tube I has an image to subject ratio of about 1 to 1.3, meaning that the subject is only 1.3 times larger than its image captured on film. Tube III has a 2.75 to 1 ratio.

Since depth of field is extremely small using a close-up system, focusing is critical. A framer is an excellent aid since a subject even a fraction of an inch too close or far away would be out of focus.

The focal framer on the Un-Tension Tubes is a U-shaped frame that extends out in front of the camera and outlines the picture area with about 1/4 inch clearance at the bottom and sides. Any subject in the plane of the frame will be in focus. A half-frame like this is preferable to a full square frame since it won't cast a shadow from above and also is a little less likely to frighten the subject.

Since there is a distortion problem with using close-up systems, the aperture should be set at a small opening—

With a standard 35mm lens on the Nikonos, the photographer could not take pictures closer than 2-3/4 feet. The photo, upper left, shows the most close-up picture possible of the one-inch tiles on the side of a swimming pool. Upper right, are the Aqua-Craft Un-Tension Tubes III (1.) and I (r.). Lower left shows the picture possible with Tube III and lower right is a shot taken with Tube I.

preferably f/22—and flash or a faster film used if resulting pictures are too dark.

FILM

Choosing the right film for the shooting may make the difference between excellent photographs and badly under-or over-exposed shots. The first choice must be between color and black-and-white. Color, of course, captures more of the true look of the underwater scene, but sometimes in dark, murky water, the black-and-white film can be more adaptable and even more effective. Both the film and its processing is cheaper than color film, and so black-and-white is a good film with which to practice.

The underwater photographer should try to use the slowest film possible for the light conditions present. The slower the film, the lower the ASA number will be and the more light will be needed to expose the film. But faster film, while having the advantage of needing less light, produces a grainier finished print.

There is no special underwater film on the market for the amateur diver/photographer, so he must use ordinary film and choose the types to fit his needs. For black-and-white, if light conditions permit, use Kodak Verichrome Pan Film (ASA 125) or Kokak Plus-X Pan Film (ASA 125). For greater depths or darker waters use Kodak Tri-X Pan Film (ASA 400).

In color film, when the light is excellent and the dive shallow, or when flash is used, Kodachrome II (ASA 25) produces extremely sharp color slides with accurate color rendition. At moderate depths use Kodak Ektachrome-X (ASA 64) and under the most adverse conditions, use High Speed Ektachrome Daylight (ASA 160). The 160 film can be "pushed" in processing to ASA 400 if desired. The photographer sets his light meter and plans his shots as if he had ASA 400 film in the camera. Then he instructs the processor to push the film to this speed in developing. There are mailing envelopes for this special process available from Kodak.

When loading and unloading film in his camera, the diver must be sure that his hands are dry and that no water falls on the film. Also, a few grains of sand inside the camera could destroy a whole roll of film. Loaded cameras should never be left out in the hot sun. This can cause the film to overheat and mark or even destroy it.

LIGHT METERS

Since light can be very deceptive underwater, a submersible light meter is a must for shooting with available light. Some divers have sealed direct-reading meters in watertight jars, but this makeshift arrangement is not really necessary since there are inexpensive underwater light meters and housings on the market.

The least expensive is the Nikon acrylic housing for the Sekonic Auto-Lumi exposure meter. If the diver has a bit more money to spend, he can go into a self-contained amphibious meter like the Sekonic Marine or the Giddings Sea Meter.

FILTERS

Filters can be helpful in bringing out the warm colors on color film and enhancing the contrast of black-and-white shots. Underwater, the most widely used are the CC-R (color compensating red) filters which are classified as warming filters.

When used with black-and-white film, these filters produce whiter whites and blacker blacks. They deepen the three-dimensional look of photographs by separating objects and emphasizing shape and dimension. In color photography, red filters hold back the blues and greens while letting through more of the red, yellow, orange and brown tones. They are most effective in shallow water since below 30 feet there are not many warm colors to be found in natural light.

Using filters necessitates wider apertures since the filters reduce the amount of light which reaches the film. For this reason, filters are not effective if the lighting is very poor.

FLASH

The only thing that can capture color at depth and allow the diver to shoot in dark or murky water is flash. Flash pictures can be taken with a flashbulb unit or with electronic flash (also called a strobe). Each has distinct advantages and disadvantages. The flashgun is much less expensive at the outset than an electronic flash, but if the diver uses it often, the cost of bulbs can run much higher in the long run.

Flashbulbs usually produce more light and warmer color tones, but electronic flash' as the advantage of action-stopping capabilities plus the convenience of not having to carry and dispose of bulbs.

Flashbulbs are normally safe to use to depths of 200 feet without fear of them imploding or exploding. It is strictly a matter of personal preference whether clear or blue bulbs are used. Most photographers agree that the clear are best for distance shots since they pick up the warmer colors and tones down the blue. Blue bulbs produce colors that are less harsh in shots taken at five feet or closer. The "B" in the bulb number—such as B5 or B26—indicates the blue bulb.

Bulbs carrying the number 5 or 25 are the ordinary large-size bulbs. Bulbs numbered 6 or 26 are for focal plane shutter cameras, like the Nikonos, and the "M" designation means miniature bulbs.

There are special submersible underwater strobes on the market. An ordinary surface unit can be adapted for underwater use by housing it in plexiglas and attaching waterproof connections.

OTHER ACCESSORIES

Since, with a mask on, it is extremely difficult, if not impossible, to see through a tiny viewfinder mounted in the camera, a sports finder should be mounted on an underwater camera. These are aligned like a gun sight and allow the diver to see the scene framed as the camera will photograph it.

There are also optically corrected viewfinders which can be mounted on top of the underwater camera or housing. These are extremely accurate but are far more expensive than the sportsfinders.

If using a flashgun, the diver will need a bulb carrier. There are two common types. One is a long strap made of gum rubber with holes for each individual bulb. The other is a mesh bag with a rubber top and a flap for extracting the bulbs. Both of these will float when filled with bulbs and can be tied to the flash gun, the camera strap, or to the diver's waist strap.

MAINTENANCE AND HANDLING

Underwater camera equipment, like most precision instruments, is fragile and, if not properly maintained, it may malfunction just when the diver needs it the most. Immersion in water is especially hard on this gear, particularly if that water is salt water.

The staff of a noted professional camera repair facility observed that saltwater corrosion is the number one repair problem for underwater flash guns. They recommend that the equipment be washed thoroughly after every dive. It is not enough to spray submersible camera gear and housings lightly with fresh water, since the salt can be caught in crevices and begin its destructive action way down in the mechanism. Each piece must be rinsed under a hard spray and then left for about an hour to soak in fresh, clean water. It should then be rinsed again and wiped with a soft cloth.

All O-rings should be periodically checked for sand, moisture, and other particles which could break the seal. The rings should also be lubricated with a silicon gel or with ordinary petroleum jelly.

Equally important is proper handling of the equipment—keeping it from shocks and bumps which could break lenses and knock meters off calibration. The best piece of equipment that the author has found for protecting and carrying camera gear is the Adapt-A-Case made by Fiberbuilt Photo Products of New York City. It is a sturdy aluminum case with foam rubber padding in the lid and movable rubber partitions that can be rearranged to house each individual piece of equipment in its own protective nook. The cases come in many sizes and shapes to fit the needs of each cameraman.

NATURAL LIGHT TECHNIQUES

It is best for the beginner to start with natural or available light photography since it is simpler than flash

An Adapt-A-Case provides protection for valuable camera gear. Its foam-cushioned partitions can be rearranged to custom house each individual piece of equipment.

photography and has fewer operations about which to be concerned. However, even after the underwater photographer is proficient in his skills, he will often take natural light pictures for the effects possible with this type of shooting. Natural light photography allows him to capture the scene as he sees it, without artificial lighting or coloration. Also, interesting highlighting can be done with the natural shadows.

When the diver is using only the actual available light, he will find that he has the most light to work with when the sun is the highest and the rays penetrate most directly. This normally occurs between the hours of 10:00 AM and 2:00 PM, when the sun is perpendicular to the surface.

Before and after this period the light falls off at more and more of an angle and less light penetrates.

This does not mean that the diver should only photograph during these hours of peak sunlight. Some very interesting back-lighting and side-lighting of subjects can be done in the earlier and later hours. However, if visibility is poor and the dive deep, the diver may find he has sufficient light for natural light photography *only* during these brightest hours of the day.

The new diver/photographer should begin by taking pictures of stationary objects like coral, starfish, shipwrecks, sunken trees, etc. Or, he may wish to have his diving buddy pose motionless for him.

Even when photographing still subjects, it is extremely important for the photographer to hold himself and his camera as immobile as possible while shooting. If the finished photo has a subject and a background that are both fuzzy, the photographer probably drifted or moved his camera.

Sometimes the diver's exhalation can jiggle the camera or his exhaust bubbles can get in front of the lens and spoil the picture. He can solve this problem by holding his breath just before he snaps the shutter. But—he must be very careful not to allow himself to drift upwards while holding his breath or he could be in danger of getting an air embolism.

Besides worrying about his breathing causing camera movement, the diver must also be concerned about the water moving him. If there is a strong underwater current or the diver is in shallow water where he is affected by the surface wave action, he may have to hold onto something stationary with his free hand, brace himself, or even wrap his legs around an object on the bottom to keep from moving.

Once he has mastered the stationary shots, the diver is ready to move up to action photos like flitting fish and gliding divers. Timing is particularly important in catching a moving fish. It is far less cooperative than a fellow scuba diver who will swim through the scene again on request. Fish are easily frightened and, since a tail is much less appealing than a broadside shot of the animal, the fish must be caught before it makes a run for cover.

The diver can tell that poor photos are the result of subject movement and not camera movement if the background is in sharp focus but the subject is fuzzy.

On cameras with adjustable shutter speeds, some of the action can be stopped by using a setting of 1/250 or 1/500. This is especially necessary for fish like the royal gamma whose motion is faster than even the human eye can capture. But, more light is needed when using the fast shutter speeds and, as a result, often lighting conditions will not permit their use.

Sometimes movement in a photo may be very desirable and will emphasize the fact that the shot was taken underwater. A technique for photographing a swimming fish consists of the photographer moving his camera sideways, focusing on the fish and following it in his viewfinder as if he were using a movie camera, and then snapping the picture when he has the subject in the desired position. This is called panning. In the resulting photograph, the fish will be in perfect focus but the background and bottom will be blurred, showing the movement. This effect can be very interesting.

Another technique for showing "underwaterness" is used when photographing another scuba diver. The modeling diver should be captured on film while he is exhaling. The bubbles add much to an underwater shot and also clearly show that the picture was really taken in the water.

So that his pictures are more interesting to the viewer, the photographer should try to make them tell a story. This can be done in a single picture such as one that shows a diver feeding an urchin to several hungry little wrasse, or another in which he is spearing a huge, appetizing grouper. It can also be done with a series of pictures that tell a more involved and detailed story. In a typical series, the photographer might start with a picture of several divers suiting up on the boat, followed by a surface shot of one diver getting ready to go over the side. This could be followed by a shot from underneath as the diver breaks the surface and then several underwater pictures as the photographer traces the diver's activities. A final shot might be a picture of the diver ascending toward the surface.

Shots using the surface as a background, by the way, are very dramatic, especially if the light rays are caught just right. In addition, shots toward the surface are useful on dim days since this angle offers maximum light.

When planning a series, the diver should photograph the same pose from several different angles so that he can later choose the one he wants. If he only shoots one of each of the scenes he wants in his series, and one of these doesn't come out right, his whole series could be ruined. It is difficult to restage a shot on another day to fit into a series.

For directing the divers—and telling them where he wants them and what he wants them to do—the photographer will find a plastic slate and a grease pencil extremely handy. Although he can't tell his fish subjects what to do in the same way, he can tempt and induce them to cooperate. Feeding the fish is a good way to attract them into camera range. In salt water where sea urchins are present, the photographer need only cut open a single urchin and the little fish will flock to feed. Bigger fish are often attracted by the activity of the smaller ones and will reamin in the area long enough to be immortalized on film.

A fish subject should never be chased. The hotter the pursuit, the more uncooperative the fish will become. Rather, remain motionless and the curious fish will come in close to investigate. Some, like freshwater bluegills and saltwater wrasse, are so bold that they will actually bump into the camera, if the diver remains still. They often become fascinated by their own reflections in the camera lens and in the diver's mask.

Being familiar with the habits of the creatures can be helpful to the underwater photographer. A damselfish, for example, establishes a territory and will couragously guard it from a threatening man-fish. The photographer can take advantage of this aggressiveness by provoking the fish to come out of hiding and be photographed on the attack. Knowing where to look for photogenic creatures like lobsters and moray eels is also an asset to the diver/photographer.

Once the subject is chosen and located, its proper framing is the next technique to master. Obviously, if the head of a diver is cut off, or most of a fish is out of the pic-

Timing is particularly important in fish photography. Photo at top is an effective broadside shot of an angelfish. Photo at bottom shows what the photographer would have gotten if he shot only a second or two, too late.

ture, the shot was improperly framed. But, in addition to avoiding these blatant mistakes, the photographer should try to plan creatively framed shots like a diver framed with coral on three sides of the photograph. If photos are consistently out of line, the frame finder should be checked for accuracy.

Because the underwater world is an area that is very different and is unfamiliar to the non-diver, the photographs taken there must help the viewer to orient himself to this strange watery domain. Shooting with a background of just water will make the shot look artificial, like a shot photographed in an aquarium. It is better to include part of the bottom in the picture to make clear the position of the subjects. Of course, the background should not be too cluttered or it will overshadow the subject.

Size orientation is also of consequence in underwater photography. A picture of a single damselfish taken with a close-up lens may make the tiny creature look five feet long, while, on the other hand, an exciting and adventurous shot of a giant Great White Shark would lose its impact if the viewer had no way of judging its size. Since everyone is familiar with the relative size of a person, a diver in the photo solves this problem. In macrophotography, a hand could be artistically placed in the picture.

No matter how well the diver may compose his photograph, it will never be a good shot unless the exposure is correct. On a snapshot camera with an electric eye, aperture is set automatically, but on an adjustable camera the photographer must choose the correct f stop which will give him just the exposure for his shot.

For available-light photography, a light meter is a must. The photographer should be sure to check his meter reading before each and every shot since the light conditions could change as much as two f stops from a cloud passing overhead. Also, a shot with the white sand bottom as a background will need much less light than one taken against a shadowy coral rock.

To be certain that he has at least one good exposure, the beginner should bracket his shots. This means that he takes three identical pictures—one at the f stop indicated by his light meter, and one on each side of it. For example, if his reading indicated an aperture of f/11, he should take the first shot at f/11, a second at f/8 and a third at f/16.

It is wise for the beginner to keep an exposure logbook. In this book he can enter the shutter speed, f stop and distance setting for each picture he takes. These three readings can be taken underwater, noted on a slate with a grease pencil, and later transferred to the book. Other notes about the dive location, lighting conditions and visibility could also be included. Then, if the diver finds that his pictures are coming out too light, he could use a faster shutter speed or a smaller lens opening. If they are too dark, the solution would be a slower shutter speed or a larger lens opening.

Practice makes perfect, so the new underwater photographer should experiment with angles, shadows and lighting until he has learned what he can do with his camera. He must also remember to have patience. Many a professional photographer has used up a full tank of air, crouching on the bottom to get one good picture.

FLASH TECHNIQUES

The underwater photographer will next want to experiment with flash. He will find that the techniques for flashguns and for electronic flash are nearly identical.

Flash can be used in a number of ways. It can serve as the primary light source when there is not enough available light for a good exposure. With color film, it can be used to bring out the warm colors which are filtered at depth. It can also provide fill-in lighting to remove shadows, add highlights, and increase contrast.

To determine the proper f stop when using flash as the primary light source, take the normal above-water guide number for the combination of film and flashbulb or electronic flash, and divide it by three. For example, if the normal guide number on the surface would be 150, use 50 underwater. But then, the diver must remember to divide this guide number by the actual camera-to-subject distance, which is approximately 25 percent farther than it appears. The camera, like the human eye, sees the subject closer, but the light from the flash must travel the actual distance to the subject. It is a good idea to bracket these shots and experiment a little with the exposures since the guide number divisor of three is only an approximation.

One of the commonest problems resulting from the use of flash is a condition called scattering. Tiny white particles dot the picture, making the scene look like the fish are swimming in a howling snow storm. This occurs because the light from the flash hits the numerous bits of plankton and silt in the water and bounces back into the lens. Scattering can be avoided by positioning the flash forward and to one side of the lens, preferably at about a 45 degree angle.

Glass is another substance that deflects the light from the flash back into the camera lens. A reflection from the mask can ruin a picture. But, if the flash is held so that the light does not hit the glass directly, it can be used effectively to light up the interior of the mask and show the diver's face.

There are several such fill-in flash techniques that can improve photos even when there is sufficient natural light for a good exposure. The flash can soften or remove harsh

Scattering is the effect of having the flash attachment too close to the camera lens. The light bounces off the particles in the water and makes the little butterfly fish look like it is out in a snowstorm.

shadows. Conversely, it can add interesting shading to an otherwise flat picture.

A fill-in technique called zone lighting is useful for emphasizing the principal subject or one specific object in a picture. If the object to be featured is in the background, hold the light high and at an angle illuminating just the back part of the scene. The foreground will be dimmer, giving the photograph a 3-D effect.

If the highlighted item is in the foreground, aim the flash low. This will result in a dark background. When the subject is photographed against only water, the background will come out nearly black—even in a color shot.

Flash makes possible pictures of those wary creatures like lobsters and eels who lurk in dark crevices. When shooting one of these creatures hidden in the coral, the flash can be placed between the coral ledge and the subject. This will highlight the animal and frame it in the blacklighted coral.

MOVIE PHOTOGRAPHY AND EQUIPMENT

Still photography does capture the beauty and fascination of the reef and the pond. But, to really bring the viewer into the underwater world, and allow him to feel its graceful, flowing motion and observe its quick-moving occupants, a movie camera is necessary.

The underwater movie photographer will encounter the same basic environmental problems as the still photographer. The solutions for problems such as color loss and refraction are the same techniques as those used by the still photographer. Therefore, an aspiring underwater cinematographer would do well to also read the preceding material in this chapter.

There are no amphibious movie cameras on the market as yet, but most any movie camera can be used underwater if put in a proper housing. Choosing a housing for a movie camera is exactly the same as selecting one for a still camera. Basically, the same features are found in each. Only the controls are different.

The amateur underwater moviemaker should choose a Super 8 camera. The next step up is 16mm which can be shown in movie theatres and even blown up to 35mm size.

Although there are no submersible underwater movie cameras, Eumig has a cast aluminum-alloy housing, specially designed for its Viennette III camera. Above, a diver holds the compact unit.

The equipment is extremely expensive, plus the cost of film and processing is at least twice and sometimes as much as four times as expensive as Super 8. Since the amateur will usually be showing to small groups, Super 8—with an audience capacity of up to 400 people—should meet his needs.

A step downward from Super 8 is 8mm but, unless he already has an 8mm camera that he must use, the diver should stay away from these. 8mm cameras are generally unacceptable for underwater work since they are usually springdriven and must be rewound by hand. Also, the spool requires turning every 25 feet and so the diver must surface, open the camera and housing, and turn the film, after only having shot half of it.

The Super 8 camera takes a film cartridge which allows the photographer to shoot 50 feet of film without having to turn the spool. This cartridge permits instant drop-in loading and protects the film from wet hands.

Super 8 frames have a 50 percent larger image area than 8mm. This provides more image detail and produces brighter projection.

Most Super 8 cameras have electric drives. With a 50 foot roll of film, this provides around three and a half minutes of continuous shooting without rewinding. Sequences are rarely that long, but at least the diver won't miss important action because of manually winding his camera when it happens.

The photographer will also find electric eyes in many Super 8 cameras. With this automatic exposure control, the diver need only check the gauge that is visible through the lens opening. It will tell him, before he shoots, if he has enough natural light or if movie lights are needed.

For providing artificial light, the diver can buy either self-contained battery-operated movie lights or surface supplied models. The self-contained units allow greater freedom of movement since the surface supplied models power their lights via a long cable from a surface generator. Often an amateur will be diving in areas and from boats where surface power is not available for his movie lights, therefore the self-contained lights are best for him. These are usually 100 to 350 watt lights encased in housings tested to 300 feet and the bulbs are color-balanced.

For movies, color film should always be used unless the light is absolutely too dim for color, or the cinematographer is striving for a special effect. There are three types of color film suitable for underwater work. Kodachrome II (ASA 40) is excellent for shallow shooting in clear water. Ektachrome, which has an ASA rating of 60, is used for dimmer light and deeper dives. There is a new high-speed film called Ektachrome 160, which is rated at ASA 160 when used without a camera filter, and has a rating of ASA 100 with the standard built-in filter present in most automatic eye cameras. This film can be used only in cameras which are capable of exposing film at these settings.

MOVIE-MAKING TECHNIQUES

The movie photographer cannot crop his pictures to change the framing, so careful viewing through a sportsfinder or viewfinder is essential. He does have the advantage of being able to edit his film. This means that bad sequences can be removed and the order of the action can be rearranged to present a more flowing story. Rarely will the underwater movie photographer show unedited film.

Because of the fact that he is able to edit, the photographer should never be afraid of shooting too much of a sequence. He can always cut some of it out, but if he doesn't have enough footage, he is either out of luck, or must restage the action—if possible. As one veteran movie photographer put it, "When you think you have more than enough of a subject—shoot a few feet more."

Not shooting enough is the mistake most often made by the beginner. After he has developed his first few movies, he will realize that a subject captured in only a few frames is totally missed by the audience, and a film full of these too-short scenes will leave the viewers dizzy and disappointed. His first tries at film-making will graphically show the need to shoot more of everything.

Since there already is motion and action in a movie, keeping the camera still is doubly important. Camera movement will detract from the action, and is very annoying to a viewer.

When shooting from a stationary position, the diver should be a little heavy—perhaps two or three pounds negatively buoyant—so that he will be stable. Like the still photographer, he must be careful of his bubbles which can vibrate the camera or get in front of the lens. Since his shooting is of longer duration than the still photographer's single "click", he must be extremely careful if he attempts to hold his breath. During a long sequence, he could unknowingly drift upward and get an embolism.

The diver will often be shooting while moving. This ability to move freely in any direction—up, down, sideways, diagonally—is a great advantage he has over the moviemaker on land, who can only achieve this mobility with the aid of costly boom equipment.

When shooting while swimming, the diver should try not

to rotate his hips, but rather swim levelly and evenly. Shots while ascending can be made with less camera movement if the diver is slightly light and can ascend without vigorous kicking.

The underwater photographer doesn't need a zoom lens since he can more effectively produce his own zoom. To zoom in on a subject, all he has to do is swim slowly, steadily, and smoothly forward while shooting. To get a very even, short-distance zoom, the diver should swim hard to build up speed before he starts filming. Then, as he turns the camera on, he can use the glide from his forward thrust to give him the motion for his zoom.

A zoom should continue right up to the subject if possible. If the final frames turn out to be too close or they exceed the close-up ability of the lens and are therefore out of focus, that final segment can always be edited out.

Zooming out, or back, is much more difficult, since a diver normally cannot swim backwards as easily and smoothly as he can swim forward. Plus, he may inadvertently photograph his own fins because of his awkward position.

A movie photographer shoots "Crist of the Abyss", an underwater statue in Florida's Pennekamp State Park. He swims slowly, zooming out from a closeup of the statue's face.

Zooming can help the photographer tell his story and lead his audience to look at what he wants them to see. For example, in a movie featuring staghorn coral, the photographer could start near the surface with a wide shot of the whole reef area to allow the viewer to get the scene in perspective. Then he could swim straight down, zooming in on a patch of staghorn on the reef. This type of shot will not only highlight his subject, but will also give the audience a feeling of descending. Later in the sequence, he could zoom in for a closeup of one branch of the staghorn, showing the tiny polyps that have constructed the stoney coral.

Zooming out is an effective way of ending a sequence. If it is to be used at the end of the movie, or at the end of the underwater shooting, the photographer can give the audience the feeling of surfacing by swimming upwards and backwards as he shoots the bottom.

Although zooming is a sensational technique, the photographer must be careful not to use too much of it in one film or it will loose its dramatic effect and will give the audience motion-sickness.

Another expressive movie technique is called *panning*. The same technique is used on land. The photographer is stationary and he moves from side to side to cover a wide area or to follow some action. The motion must be slow and smooth, and should last at least 15 seconds. A shorter or faster sequence would resemble the sight of telephone poles from the window of a car going 40 miles an hour, and would have the audience asking "What was that?"

When panning an area, the diver should hold the camera still for a few frames at the beginning, then pan slowly, and finish with several still frames at the end of the pan. This will help him make smooth transitions from one scene to the next when editing the film.

The photographer can capture the motion of fish or other divers with zooming or panning techniques, but sometimes it is equally effective to stay in one spot and allow the subject to swim in and out of the camera range. The photographer should shoot a few seconds of film after the subject has passed out of the scene, before he moves to another sequence. As with panning, this extra film will smooth transitions.

Movement in any direction is possible while shooting underwater. The diver should use this ability to get angle shots—circling his subject, getting under it and over it. There is no end to the creative shots a diver can achieve with just a little imagination and his underwater weightlessness.

Cut-away scenes can be very interesting in a film. For example, the photographer might show divers working on the bottom, then cut to a scene of two more divers swimming down from the surface, and finally cut back to the working divers. Or, when editing the film, he could even cut away to a surface sequence, such as the activity in the dive boat during a film of the divers swimming below.

Overlapped action is another editing technique. The photographer shows the same scene from two views. For example, he may shoot a diver on the surface, filming him as he rolls over the side of the boat and hits the water. The next sequence, shot from underwater, would show the unrippled surface suddenly broken by the diver's entry and the cameraman would then follow the diver down.

Obviously, the photographer cannot be in two places at once, so shots like this must be staged. The diving subject would have to make two entries so that the photographer could capture both views.

Like the still photographer, the underwater moviemaker must be concerned with light. Movies usually come out best when the scene is front-lighted. Therefore, when using natural light, the diver should try to keep the sun behind him and have it hit his subjects head-on. When using movie lights, it is easy to front-light a subject, but, as with a flash, the lights must be mounted far enough from the lens to avoid scattering.

It has been noted that a series of prints or a slide show should tell a story. This is even more essential in moviemaking. Before the dive, the movie photographer should have at least a general idea of the story he wants to tell. He may even want to develop a loose script and coach his diving actors and actresses beforehand. In an unfamiliar area, or when shooting fish life, a script or even a loose outline may be impossible. In that case, the photographer can shoot at random, building up his library of footage. Later, these sequences can be edited into story form or used as fill-ins for other movies.

Of course, the diver must be flexible. If while following a story plan, he spots a huge manta ray, his plan should be aborted while he shoots this beautiful creature which is so seldom seen.

When developing a diving story, the photographer should include some surface shots, especially when non-divers will be among those in his audience. In a film on the building of an artificial reef of tires, for example, the photographer Dean May began with footage of processing and preparing the tires on land, followed by scenes of their loading in one of the boats. At the drop site, he entered the water and, while treading water near the boat, shot a sequence of the boatmen tossing the tires overboard. Then he submerged to record them breaking the surface and crashing down around him. The tires were ultimately followed down to their resting place. Months later, he returned to the site to photograph the now established tires, record the marine growth on them and shoot the fish life that had come to inhabit the new reef.

This filming resulted in a movie that is interesting to divers but also informative to the non-diver, which leads to one final, important point. If the diver plans on showing his underwater photography to others—whether he is shooting stills or movies—he must consider the non-diver as well as his fellow divers. This will result in more people enjoying and understanding his work. Plus, he will be doing his part to introduce others to the wonderful underwater world.

3 Diving for Treasure

THE OCEAN IS the largest treasure chest in the world. From the early 1500s to the late 18th century, European ships put to sea carrying gold, silver, jewels and other valuables between the New World and the Old. Many of these cargoes found their way to the bottom, when the ships fell victim to foul weather, treacherous reefs and pirate attacks.

Spain, for example, shipped an average of 17 million pesos a year for a period of nearly 300 years, and about 10% of it ended up on the ocean floor.

In more modern times, weather, mechanical failure, human error and war have sunk hundreds of craft ranging from pleasure yachts to submarines. These, too, carried valuable cargoes and personal effects to the ocean bed.

In addition to being a repository for treasure, the ocean is also a historical museum displaying the technology, art and life style of short periods of history, capsulized in a sunken ship or even a suddenly flooded city.

These treasures and artifacts have lain undisturbed for many years, since they were inaccessible to the world's greatest destroyer of the past—man. They were protected by an environment in which he could not breathe. But man is inventive, and with such riches waiting to reward his efforts, he began looking for ways to conquer the watery depths.

As early as the era of the ancient Greek city-states, divers of Rhodes used hollow reeds as their only breathing equipment to salvage vessels that sunk in the harbor. They were rewarded by the ship's owner with a percentage of the worth of the materials recovered. The diver kept one-half of what he retrieved if the shipwreck was in over 22 feet of water, one-third in 12 to 22 feet, and one-tenth in less than 12 feet.

In 1663, an efficient breathing apparatus was used by Colonel Hans Albrecht von Treileben to recover more than 50 bronze cannons from the Swedish gunboat Vasa, which sunk in Stockholm harbor on her maiden voyage. The Colonel used the newly perfected diving bell. The heavy iron bell, suspended on a cable, was dropped to the bottom, full of air from the surface. The diver, inside the cavity of the bell, used this air. The air was renewed by sinking air-filled casks lower than the bell, then opening them and allowing the air to escape up into the cavity.

A rather bizarre recovery method was devised by the Japanese a hundred years ago. A boatload of the Emperor's valuable vases sunk in the Sea of Japan and settled in water too deep for free diving. So, the resourceful divers captured live octopuses, tied lines on them, and dropped them over the site of the lost vases. The terrified creatures, looking for someplace to hide, immediately slid into the jars. Then the lines were pulled in, bringing jar and octopus up together—the art treasure for the Emperor and the succulent octopus for the divers' dinner tables.

Salvage and treasure diving became more practical and profitable with the invention of the "closed dress" helmet diver's suit, consisting of a watertight dress, weighted shoes and belt, and a windowed helmet which received air via a hose from a surface compressor. But this was, and still is, a costly and restrictive unit, out of the reach of the amateur.

It wasn't until the advent of scuba gear that the real age of underwater archeology began. Hundreds of men and women donned this new diving gear to probe beneath the sea—and many of them found treasure. In fact, most of the major treasures and archeological finds have been the discoveries of sport divers.

Initially, these divers did not realize the extent of the underwater treasure they discovered. Often, they picked up a few cannons and pieces of eight, not knowing that an entire ship lay buried beneath the sand. Once they removed the surface artifacts which marked the site, this location was lost, perhaps forever.

The excavation of the English frigate *Looe* in Florida in 1951 was a landmark in the history of underwater archeology. Here, for the first time, historical research was combined with exploration of an underwater site. Commander Mendel Peterson of the Smithsonian Institution worked with the divers to identify and record their find.

Since then, many divers have taken the trouble to find out the right way to work a treasure site. Historians and professional archeologists are realizing what a valuable worker the amateur diver can be. In fact, just as volunteers work with scientists at archeological digs on land, sport divers are now working side by side with professionals underwater. In the summer of 1972, an affiliate of the Smithsonian Institution called Educational Expeditions International (EEI) of Boston, Mass. gathered a group of 23 sport divers to excavate a 17th century shipwreck off the coast of Bermuda. These divers worked under the direction of Commander Mendel Peterson and the renowned treasure diver, Teddy Tucker. Due to the success of this venture, EEI is planning several of these expeditions a year, for divers who want to "be where it's at" in underwater archeology.

For the diver not joining an expedition but working on his own with other amateurs, this chapter will outline proper procedures for finding, excavating, and recording shipwrecks and other treasure sites. Thus, the diver can benefit fully from all the treasures to be found in the ocean, whether he dives once a week, during his vacation, or only occasionally.

The landlocked diver will not be forgotten, since fresh water often yields the best preserved artifacts. Techniques for treasure diving in the ocean can be used by the lake, spring or quarry diver as well.

WHERE TO LOOK

There are basically four types of underwater treasure sites. The first is the refuse site, an underwater accumulation of artifacts near a former camp site, village or town. The second is the shrine. Tribal people, particularly in Mexican and Central American areas, often tossed jewels, gold, and sometimes human sacrifices into a particular lake or spring that they deemed "holy." The Mayan sacred well at the ruins of Chichen Itza in Yucatan yielded priceless gold and silver ornaments.

The third type of site is the submerged town which was flooded suddenly by an earthquake, tidal wave or hurricane. The "sin city" of Port Royal, for example, slid into what is now the Bay of Kingston, Jamaica, as the result of a violent earthquake on June 7, 1692.

The fourth site, and the one most popular with the scuba diver, is the shipwreck. Since it is the easiest for the amateur diver to find and salvage, the exploration of this kind of site will be stressed in this chapter.

Shipwrecks may be found all over the world, in almost every sea, but the greatest concentration of wrecks is, of course, along major shipping routes. The route of the 16th, 17th and 18th century treasure ships wound among the islands of the Caribbean, continued on up the eastern coast of Mexico and touched at Bermuda.

Bermuda is rich in shipwrecks since it was the final landmark for sailing back to Europe. The sailors used this sighting to pick up the westerly winds. But often they ventured too close to the jagged reefs and instead, ended their journey beneath Bermuda's indigo waters.

The coastal waters of Florida contain more wrecks than any other region of the United States. This fact, coupled with the warm, clear waters of the area, makes Florida the world's main center for underwater treasure hunting.

The Bahamas are also popular with American divers because of the crystal-clear water and the close proximity of the islands to our mainland. Many virgin wrecks are awaiting discovery, particularly along the out islands.

Fresh waters can harbor excellent shipwrecks. While the wrecks are not as numerous, they are found in far better condition than saltwater wrecks. An ancient craft more than a century old was raised from Lake Champlain with the wood still intact. The Great Lakes is the greatest freshwater graveyard of vessels, especially Lake Michigan off the northwestern coast of the state of Michigan.

After one of these regions, or any other general area, has been chosen, the search can be further narrowed down to the reefs, sandbars and other obstacles to navigation in the area. Even if these impediments did not cause the wreck, the ship often was steered or driven onto them before it sank.

There are two ways of locating wrecks. One is to search at random, and then attempt to identify and evaluate the find. The second is to do extensive research, pinpoint the location of a desirable wreck and then set out to find it. The best method is probably a compromise between the two, in which the diver studies the available information to become familiar with all the recorded wrecks of a small area, locates a wreck, and then does further research to identify it.

Where does the diver go for information? Records on Spanish ships are found in the Archieves of the Indies in Seveille, Spain and those on English ships in the Public Records Office in London. Insurance companies which write marine insurance are also valuable sources. Lloyds of London insured many of the early ships and included brief accounts of lost vessels in "Lloyd's List," their newspaper on British shipping.

For shipwrecks that occurred after the mid-1800s, newspapers, ship's logs, court-martial records, and local history books are helpful.

Names of places can be clues, too. For instance, the reef on which the wreck of the *Looe* rested was identified on the charts as "Looe Reef," long before the wreck was discovered. Even if the name of a wreck is not in evidence, names like Wreck Hill, Cannon Inlet or Bloody Bay are good indications that a shipwreck occurred there.

Charts of the coastal U.S., marking known wrecks and indicating varying depths, can be obtained from the Director, U.S. Coast and Geodetic Survey, Dept. of Commerce, Washington, D. C. For similar charts of the Great Lakes, write to the U.S. Army Corps of Engineers, Lake Survey, 630 Federal Building, Detroit, MI.

LOCATING THE WRECK

Although romantic stories of shipwrecks picture the derelict vessel completely intact, resting on the bottom at a slight list, with the skeleton of the ill-fated captain still lashed to the wheel, this is almost never the case. When a ship sinks in the ocean, it settles into the sand. Almost immediately part of it is buried. The wood that is above the sand line is quickly inhabited by teredo worms who take their first little nibbles.

Over the months, currents, tides and weather shift the ship and its cargo. Coral begins to grow on the wood and metal, encrusting and cementing together the small items. Sea fans, gorgonian coral and anemone camouflage the wreck to resemble a colorful sea garden.

By the time the sea has completed its work, little more than a pile of ballast stones or a few cannons may be visible. The job of the diver searching for a treasure ship is therefore a difficult one.

There are numerous search methods. The best one to use depends on water clarity and conditions, weather, finances and many other factors. The simplest method is the visual search. In flat calm seas where the water is gin-clear and the visibility between 100 and 200 feet, wrecks have been located by a watcher standing on the bow of the boat and keeping an eye out for anything unusual. The impression of a straight line or a sharp right angle may give away the location of a shipwreck since these are never natural underwater. In some cases, part of the coral encrusted vessel may be visible, or cannon and ballast stones may give away its hiding place.

The bottom could be surveyed through a glass-bottom

boat, with a glass-bottom bucket held over the side of a slow-moving vessel, or by a diver pulled behind the boat on a sea sled. Most recently, visual search has been made easier with the use of small, slow-moving, light planes. A seaplane or pontoon-rigged helicopter has the advantage of being able to land on the water when something is sighted.

Teddy Tucker has even used a balloon to carry him over the calm Bermudian waters while he looked for signs of shipwrecks. This method is most effective if the balloon is equipped with a portable marine radio and the searcher can communicate with a boat below.

In more murky waters, such as along the northeastern coast of the U.S., grappling is a simple search method often used. The boat is guided slowly over a set course, while a grapple hook on a line is dropped over the stern and dragged. As soon as something is hooked, a diver is sent down to investigate. If it is worthwhile, he attaches a marker buoy and the boat is anchored for a more thorough look. Unfortunately, this method is useful only in areas with a smooth sand bottom, free from entangling sea weed or large craggy rocks.

An excellent marker buoy can be made from a plastic bleach bottle, some strong twine, and a weight of about three to five pounds. Cap the bottle securely and tie one end of a 100-foot length of twine to the handle. Wrap the twine around the body of the bottle and tie a weight to the other end. When the buoy is tossed overboard the twine will rapidly spin and unwind and the weight will hold the unit in place.

When two vessels are available for the search, a sweep cable can be slung between them and dragged on the bottom. As soon as something is snagged, a pair of divers go down to check it out. A larger area can be covered quickly with this dragging method.

If a small area is pinpointed, the divers can initiate a swimmer's search. The boat is moored and an anchor line dropped. A diver attaches a 1/4 inch nylon line approximately 100 feet long to the anchor chain. This line must be knotted at regular intervals, close enough so the diver can see from one knot to the next.

A pair of divers swim out to the end of the rope and plant a small stake in the sand. Swimming in a full circle, they search the area within their view. When they return to the stake, they remove it, move down to the next knot, and repeat the procedure until the 100-foot radius circle is completely covered. In any type of swimmer's search, it is vital that no spot be overlooked, therefore hit-and-miss swimming without a line is ineffective.

From the simplicity of the swimmer's search the diver can go all the way to using advanced electronic search equipment, ranging in price from less than a hundred dollars to many thousands of dollars. The simplest piece of equipment to operate is the depth finder, which indicates depth read at a single point beneath the boat.

The most desirable type is the recording depth finder which marks the depth on scaled paper every fraction of a minute, resulting in a drawing of the ocean floor. During a search for wrecks, one person is assigned to watch the recorder. At the instant an unusually high point is noticed, the watcher shouts for a marker buoy to be immediately tossed overboard. Then the boat can circle, returning to the exact spot in order to send a pair of divers down.

A more sophisticated type of depth recorder is the scanner. It can read a greater area of bottom, as its beam swings in an arc like a pendulum. This unit covers an area faster and avoids the possibility of missing a wreck site by a few feet, since the terrain is recorded most thoroughly.

To find a wreck completely covered by sand or silt, which would therefore not register on a depth recorder, a magnetometer or metal detector can be used. Underwater models are available with a detection head which can be towed behind a boat and which will detect ferrous objects from as far as up to fifty feet away. Smaller handheld models can be used in a swimmer's search.

The weekend diver may want to explore wrecks that have already been discovered. For these, Loran numbers may be available. Loran is a navigational system which operates by taking two numerical readings at the intersection of two pairs of radio signals, in order to pinpoint a position on the open sea. This is an indispensable instrument for relocating wreck sites which are out of sight of land but not marked with a permanent buoy.

When the wreck is close inshore, its position can be marked by land bearings (see illustration). Land bearings are useful since whenever two objects on the shore are lined up, only one straight line can be drawn through them. To pinpoint a location at sea, two sets of these pairs of objects must be located whose lines intersect directly over the wreck site—preferably at a 90 degree angle. The objects chosen should be highly visible and easily spotted such as a water tower, a church steeple, or the peak of a pointed roof. The farther apart the two objects are, the more definitive will be the line drawn through them.

To locate a wreck, the captain lines up one set of bearings and then runs in toward shore until the other set lines up. As soon as this point is reached, a marker buoy should be dropped. Then the boat can swing around and anchor near the buoy.

SETTING UP AND SURVEYING THE SITE

First, a permanent buoy should be set by firmly attaching a chain to a coral head or other stable bottom feature and fixing a buoy to the other end of the chain. Then, lines can be tied directly to this buoy, instead of having to anchor the boat each time it is brought to the work site.

Before any excavation work is begun, the entire site must be surveyed to see if it is economically feasible to excavate, to determine the type of tools needed and to estimate the size and shape of the wreck. It should be remembered that valuable objects are often scattered far from the hull sections, so a wide perimeter must be surveyed. As the divers swim over the wreck for this study, they should also

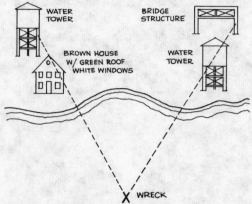

BEARING #1
LINE UP THE RIGHT LEG OF THE BRIDGE STRUCTURE WITH THE
LEFT LEG OF THE WATER TOWER

BEARING #2
LINE UP THE PEEK OF THE ROOF OF THE HOUSE WITH THE RIGHT
LEG OF THE WATER TOWER

AT THE POINT WHERE THESE TWO BEARINGS CROSS IS THE
WRECK

A sample of a land bearings map for locating an inshore wreck.

determine its condition. Is it buried in sand or encrusted in coral? How much of it is buried? What is the state of the visible materials?

Once work has begun, divers should not spearfish in the surrounding water nor throw garbage over the side of the boat. These activities attract sharks and barracuda.

The site must be recorded before it is touched, particularly since artifacts removed from the spot of original discovery may lose their context if their position was not noted before they were raised. A combination of photography and mapping provides the most thorough working plan.

Excellent photographs of the site can be compiled using a simple underwater camera such as the Nikonos. The only special equipment needed is a spirit level and a plumb line attached to the camera to keep it horizontal and at a fixed distance from the bottom. The diver swims slowly in a straight line snapping pictures at regular intervals. The

With her slate weighted down by a piece of coral rock, a diver proceeds to map a wreck site.

finished photos can be trimmed and put together to form a composite of the site.

For underwater mapping, all that is needed is a sheet of acetate plastic and an ordinary graphite pencil. The diver positions himself on the bottom and draws one section at a time. First, a compass reading is taken and noted on the slate. All artifacts, all changes in terrain, and all natural objects such as coral heads are drawn. Actual duplication of the objects is not necessary but their precise location and inclusion of all details is vital.

To obtain the most accurate mapping, a grid system can be set up. This means marking off the area in equal size squares, then giving each of the lines in one direction a number designation and each of the intersecting lines a letter designation. The grid may be laid out using ropes, lines or wire; or a prefabricated grid can be dropped by light cables.

Mendel Peterson developed an easy way of mapping a wreck using an azimuth circle. This bearing circle is mounted on a brass rod or tripod which is driven into the bottom at the approximate center of the wreck. This becomes the point from which all subsequent measurements are taken. Using a magnetic compass, the azimuth circle is lined up with magetic north. A chain is connected to the center of the circle and distances are marked on the chain.

When an item is to be put on the map, the diver stretches the chain to the object and notes its bearing on the azimuth circle and its distance from the brass rod, as read from the marks on the chain. With these two readings a pinpoint location can be made.

BREATHING APPARATUS

The initial equipment to choose is the type of breathing apparatus. This decision is affected primarily by the depth of the wreck. When working a wreck in 30 feet of water or less that is confined to a relatively small area, scuba gear can be used, but surface supplied air is more efficient. With this type of equipment, the diver can stay down for hours without having to come up and change tanks.

The two most widely used units are Desco and Hookah. Both use a surface compressor that pumps air through a long rubber hose to the diver. The difference between the two is that the Hookah rig feeds the air into a demand regulator, similar to the type used on a tank, while the Desco has a full face mask with an adjustable constant air flow. With the Desco the diver can breathe through his nose as well as his mouth.

In deeper water and where the wreck has protrusions or lines which may cut or snag surface air hoses, scuba gear is more practical. For extended exposure necessitating decompression, or if the diver is going inside the wreck, a pony bottle should be worn for emergencies. A pony bottle is a small tank with a capacity of 5 to 15 cu. ft. of air, equipped with a separate regulator. It can be attached to a single tank or a set of doubles.

Because of the hazards, complications and bottom time limitations of working in very deep water, the amateur diver should confine his unsupervised wreck diving to shallower sites, particularly if he is going to excavate or perform any heavy work.

EXCAVATION

If the wreck is completely or partially covered with sand or silt, this overburden must be removed. One way of doing this is to use an airlift, which is basically a long open tube into which compressed air is pumped. The air enters the tube near the bottom and is blown toward the surface, causing a suction which lifts up surface sand and silt.

The suction can be varied by a control valve on the air hose. Also, the larger the diameter of the tube, the stronger the suction will be. A 6-inch air lift is powerful and is used only to remove overburden. Smaller air lifts—also called sand guns—can be used in "pay dirt" where the sand is filled with small valuable objects. The sand is gently lifted while the operator or an assistant picks up the uncovered items.

Small items can be retrieved by feeding the exhaust of the airlift into a barge or floating screen where they can be sifted out and recovered. Or, if the water is very clear, the tube can be exhausted underwater with a watcher posted to catch any item inadvertently sucked up the tube.

The operator of the air lift should work on the leeward side of the underwater tidal currents so that the fallout will be carried away from the wreck. If the tide is coming from the north, he should begin on the far south perimeter of the site. Sand should be exhausted and piled off the wreck site or at least into previously excavated areas.

An airlifting tool can be easily constructed (see illustration) and used with a compressor located in the boat. If a compressor is not available, the boat's propeller can supply the power to remove overburden. A prop-wash is a unit as simple to make and operate as the air-lift (see illustration). It consists of an elbow-shaped metal tube, usually aluminum, that is fitted over the prop and attached to the boat's transom. The vessel is moored with four anchors. Then the engine is started and its speed varied, depending on the depth of water and the amount of sediment to be removed.

The wash of the propeller is forced into the tube, creating a whirlpool action. This pushes clear water to the bottom at a high velocity and blasts away sand or silt rapidly. The deeper the water, the wider will be the diameter of the excavated area. The prop-wash is

Divers excavating a Bermuda wreck site, use a small air lift with an underwater exhaust.

The suction of the air lift digs a hole in the sand and also kicks up tasty tidbits for a hungry parrot fish.

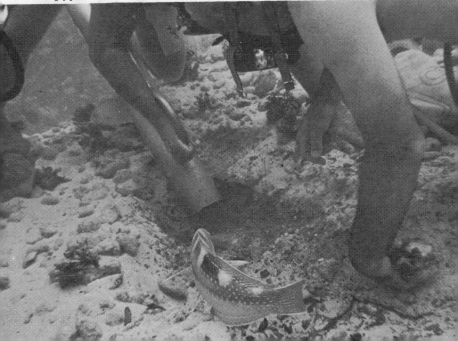

(Photo courtesy of Underwater Archaeological Associates, Inc.)
A prop wash unit is carried behind the dive boat. When in operation, it swings upside down so that the tube curves downward.

powerful and must be properly controlled or it will wash away artifacts and even break up wood.

Sometimes the diver may find that in addition to being covered with sand, parts of the wreck are heavily encrusted in coral. He can plant charges to blast the coral apart, but this often destroys what is inside and also kills fish in the immediate area. It is slower, but far better to use chisels and hammers to chip the coral apart. There are air chisels and hammers that can be used underwater which will speed up this operation. Large chunks can be broken loose, taken to the surface and there slowly and carefully taken apart.

High pressure water-jets can be used to blast coral apart, too. A water-jet is nothing more than a hose fitted with a special underwater recoilless jetting nozzle. A pump forces water out with enough power to crumble the coral. The drawback of this unit is that it destroys underwater visibility.

Once the wreck has been excavated down to a very light cover of sand, hand fanning works well to recover small objects. The sand is gently fanned with the hand or a flat object like a ping pong paddle.

LIFTING

Small items can be gathered in a close mesh or canvas "goodie bag" and brought to the surface. For larger items, the diver needs more than his own muscle power. If his boat is equipped with a crane, power winch or lifting tackle, these can be used to raise heavy objects.

The cheapest and simplest lifting method is the use of compressed air floatation gear, which can be lifting bags or metal tanks. The empty bag or tank is submerged, attached to the object to be lifted, and then filled with compressed air from an auxiliary tank or the diver's regulator. Air displaces the water inside making the entire unit buoyant and raising it to the surface.

Thus employed for big jobs, the 55-gallon steel drum offers a lifting power of about 400 lbs. The drum should have four holes punched just beneath the lip and a heavy line spliced or shackled through each hole. These four lines are gathered together and tied to a ring. The object to be lifted can be tied directly to the ring or put in a sling. If more than 400 lbs of lifting power is needed, several drums can be lashed together.

For smaller jobs, canvas or rubberized lifting bags of various sizes are available. These, like the drums, must be open at the bottom so that expanding air can bleed out as the bag rises. When the diver is working with a lifting device he must be warned to stay clear of it or it may take him on a fast, uncontrolled and possibly fatal ascent. The diver should never put his head in the bag and exhale to inflate it, for it is too easy to get tangled in the ropes. The device should be filled with air until it slowly starts for the surface, and then be released. It will accelerate rapidly on the way up.

When the bag or drum breaks the surface, it can be hooked by crew members in the boat and pulled in. Or, if the object is too big and drums are used, it may be floated to shore behind the boat.

All finds, large and small, that are brought up should be recorded together with the date salvaged, the original location and the condition of the item noted.

IDENTIFYING THE WRECK

Learning the name, nationality and age of a wreck can be a very difficult task. On a modern wreck it is easier, since the name is often engraved on the ship's bell, silverware and other items and may even still be discernible on the hull. With older wrecks identification takes much more work. For these ships, amateur divers are advised to consult experts who may be found in local museums and also in archeology and history departments of universities. Items from the wreck can be brought or sent to them for identification.

Coins are excellent clues to discovering the age of a wreck, particularly if large numbers of them are found bearing the same date or a short span of dates. Obviously, the ship sank sometime after the date of the newest coin. The condition of the coins should be studied to determine if, and how long, they have been in circulation, thus narrowing the range of years. Coins are not useful, however, for establishing the nationality of a wreck since sailors car-

Cannons are often used to identify shipwrecks. Above is one from the *HMS Winchester* lost on September 24, 1695 and salvaged in 1938.

ried coins of many nations. Also, large shipments of newly-minted coins were often stolen from ships of other nations.

Cannons can tell much about a sunken ship. The trunnion frequently carried the date of casting and sometimes also the coat of arms of the monarch of the country in which the cannon was cast. When these marks are not visible, cannons can be identified by their distinctive shapes. Also the type of vessel can be recognized by the number of cannon carried.

Bottles are a valuable find. Their shapes have changed so often throughout history that they can usually be dated to within ten years. Ordnance materials are also revealing since they carried government marks. The type of wood found on a shipwreck can disclose the country in which the vessel was built. English shipbuilders used primarily pine, while Scandinavians used softwoods.

The final identification of any wreck comes from putting all the pieces of information together, consulting experts and archives, and then hoping that the shipwreck was recorded.

PRESERVATION OF ARTIFACTS

Many a diver has recovered fascinating artifacts from the sea, only to watch them disintegrate before his very eyes. The extent of the damage done to these items depends on the temperature, salinity, oxygen, mineral and acid content, and sedimentation of the water from which they came.

These objects may be brought up in one of three states: one, found in their original condition requiring little or no treatment; two, suffering some damage or chemical change which can be arrested and the remains preserved; and three, incapable of being preserved except by being encased in plastic or captured on film.

When bringing an artifact up from the site, the first rule a diver must remember is to keep the recovered object wet. If it is encrusted in coral it should be kept in salt water, otherwise fresh water is satisfactory. If it is impossible to transport the item in water, it should be taken home in an airtight container or at the very least, wrapped in airtight plastic wrap.

Gold, the dream of every treasure diver, is one of the substances that is normally recovered in a perfect state of preservation. Porcelain, hard gem stones, terra cotta and coal fall in the same category, needing only a brief wash in fresh water to remove the salts. If these items are encrusted with coral, gentle tapping with a small hammer or frequent washings in a 10% solution of nitric acid will remove it.

Lead suffers only superficial oxidation which may be removed with a 10-20% solution of acetic acid.

Iron and steel, the most abundant metals on shipwrecks, are also the most susceptible to the destruction of sea water. This is because certain metals combined with salt water form a gigantic galvanic battery. The salt acts as the electrolyte and metals of two different molecular weights form opposite poles, creating a current of electrons between them. By this process of electrolysis, iron is converted to iron oxide—more commonly known as rust.

Metal artifacts left untreated, even for a few days, will soon begin disintegrating like the pieces above.

There is no quick, one-step method of preserving iron or steel. The object must first be placed in a bath of 10% sodium hydroxide for four to six weeks. Then the solution must be renewed and mossy zinc metal added, causing bubbling within an hour or two. The object is left in this bath for three weeks and then cleaned of its white coating with a solution of 5% sulfuric acid. This is followed by freshwater baths for several weeks until the water remains clear. After drying, the object can be coated with clear lacquer, plastic spray or melted paraffin.

Electrolysis also affects silver, converting it into silver sulfide. At its worst, it can only be preserved by being encased in plastic. However, if it was in contact with a metal like iron, it may survive intact and need only a bath in 15% ammonium hydroxide and a rub with a paste of water and baking soda.

Wood is especially vulnerable and may shrink, shrivel, curl or flake if left in the open air. It must immediately be put in fresh water—preferably running water—for two to four weeks to remove all salts. Next, it should be placed in a closed container with 100% ethel alcohol 3 or 4 times the volume of the wood.

To prevent wood from shriveling, the pores must be filled. Polyethylene-glycol (known by the trade names Polywax or Carbowax) has been used effectively for this purpose. A one to one solution of polyethylene-glycol and ethyl alcohol must be mixed and heated to 65 degrees C. The wood is kept in this solution in a 65 degree oven until all the alcohol has evaporated, sometimes as long as 30 days. If a small amount of the fluid, removed from the oven, cools and hardens within an hour, then all the alcohol has evaporated. The wood should be rinsed quickly under hot water and dried with a lint-free cloth.

Not all non-treated wood will shrivel. Hardwood items, with very close grain, may survive intact after only the alcohol bath. Wood being brought up for decorative purposes may be allowed to twist into interesting shapes as it dries, but it will be very fragile.

For extremely fragile or tiny items, plastic embedding may be best. Most hobby shops carry kits of resin and a catalyst, with complete instructions for use. Variously-shaped molds can be purchased or any glass, pyrex, tin or ceramic dish used. The object must be thoroughly dry—wiped or dried in a warm oven—or the moisture will form a haze in the plastic.

Paraffin is very handy to use as a sealant. To cite an instance, diver Dean May retrieved a pair of century-old round-bottom bottles sealed with natural corks and full of the original ginger ale. To assure that the ginger ale would not seep out while the bottles were on display, Dean heated and melted paraffin in a small pan and dipped the neck of each bottle and its cork into the liquid. Upon drying and hardening, this lightly coated the cork and neck with wax and sealed the soft drink inside.

LAWS GOVERNING "FINDS"

All wrecks belong to someone and the rule of "finders keepers" very rarely applies. After the diver has salvaged a wreck and the treasure is ashore, it is too late to start checking the local laws. Divers have ended up with no treasure, stiff fines, and even jail sentences for operating (salvaging) without permission.

Salvage rights to modern shipwrecks are often held by insurance companies. The diver may either buy these rights for a nominal fee or offer his salvage services for a percentage of the profits.

In any venture, it is best to consult a *local* lawyer, well-versed in maritime law, since laws vary greatly from country to country and even from state to state. Salvage operations in any navigable U.S. waters must be cleared with the Army Corps of Engineers. The federal government has established control over a three-mile territorial limit, however, some coastal states claim jurisdiction even farther out to sea. Florida, Texas, the Carolinas and Virginia even have laws specifically covering the salvage of shipwrecks.

The number one treasure diving state in the country is also the strictest. The Florida Board of Archives and History in Tallahassee is in charge of all diving operations up to 10 miles out. The diver must first obtain an exploration permit before he can even officially begin looking. Once he locates a wreck, he must apply for a pinpoint lease. When, and if, this is granted, a marine archeologist and several conservation officers are assigned by the Board to supervise all operations. The state receives 25% of everything recovered and retains a right to purchase any or all of the diver's share.

Canada passed a stringent law in 1968 which states that no work may be conducted on any ancient shipwreck without the permission of the National Historical Park Service. Although, like Florida, Canada assigns an archeologist to supervise the work, this government has only claimed 10% of the profits in the past.

Permission to treasure dive in Mexican waters must be obtained through CEDAM (Club of Explorations and Aquatic Sports of Mexico) a group founded by Pablo Bush Romero to protect shipwrecks from being plundered. Americans can become members of this group and work on Mexican shipwrecks.

Bermuda has more shipwrecks per mile of coastline than any other area. No permit is needed to search, but new wrecks must be registered with the Receiver of Wrecks. Divers taking anything from a wreck registered to someone else are severely fined by the Bermudian government. The diver keeps anything he recovers, but the government can buy whatever it wants at a fair price established by impartial experts. This situation sounds ideal—but there is a catch. Registration of wrecks is only granted to Bermudian citizens, so if a foreign diver wants to salvage a wreck, he must go into partnership with a Bermudian.

In the Bahamas, divers wishing to salvage a wreck must obtain a permit from the Ministry of Transportation. This government is very strict about salvaging without a permit. In these islands the diver's share is 75%.

Jamaica may be a diving paradise, but it is no place for the treasure diver. The government claims 100% of all artifacts and 50% of all treasure, with the right to purchase the remaining 50% at bullion value! Columbia is nearly as bad. Although the diver gets 75%, no gold in any form can leave the country and any Columbian museum can purchase all or part of the 75% at any price considered reasonable by the museum personnel.

The rest of South America and all of Central America is free of all salvage laws. In addition, much of the sea bottom is virgin territory. Mediterranean waters are plagued with the laws of the surrounding countries. These laws vary greatly and seem to be constantly changing.

But wherever the treasure diver is operating he should try to have permission in writing from the local authorities. This document should state the diver's name, the precise vessel he will be salvaging and its location, the percentage he receives and his rights of disposal, plus any time or equipment limitations on the salvage operation.

WEEKEND TREASURE HUNTERS

The guidelines for treasure divers undertaking a full-scale excavation, apply as well to the weekend diver who visits local wrecks via charter boats or his own small craft. He, too, needs to understand the operation of depth finders and other equipment for locating wrecks. He needs to know the techniques for uncovering and raising artifacts from the vessels on which he dives. Once his find is on deck or back home, he'll want to identify it and keep it intact. For this diver, just visiting a wreck for a few dives to sightsee or bring up a souvenir of his venture, there are a few additional points to remember.

First of all, he must remember that there is no such thing as a completely picked-over wreck. No matter how many divers have been on a site, he can come up with something by hand fanning the sand around the periphery of the wreck, looking under pieces of wreckage, and just being a little more observant than the last guy.

Captain Charlie Stratton, who operates the charter boat *Bottom Time* off the New Jersey coast, always lets his passengers complete at least one dive before he enters the water. Yet, even when everyone else has come up saying there was "absolutely nothing on the wreck", Charlie comes up with all kinds of artifacts. Why? Because he is just a little more observant, diligent and experienced than most.

While being observant to look for "goodies", the diver must also swim alertly and be wary of underwater currents which can force him roughly against the shipwreck. Wrecks, particularly metal ones, are full of jagged panels, sharp cables and broken glass which can tear wet suits, cut lines and hoses, and severely cut the unwary diver.

When going inside the wreck, the diver must exercise utmost caution. A reliable light must be carried by each diver and if the diver is entering via a hatch, it should be securely tied back. The interior of a wreck is like a maze, so a life line must be secured at the entrance to the wreck and carried by the diver as he swims inside. His fins and exhaust bubbles can kick up so much silt in the compartments that his only way of getting out may be to follow the line.

When diving on an unfamiliar wreck, it is best to descend on the anchor line. This will put the diver directly on the ship and give him a point of reference.

It is one thing to bring up trophies from a wreck and quite another to be a scavenger. Destroying a virgin site for its scrap value before the wreck has been identified and recorded is a terrible waste. Besides destroying wrecks which might otherwise have been enjoyed by divers for many years, scavenging is, in most areas, illegal. Like the treasure diver of years ago who brought up the cannons and thereby obliterated all evidence identifying the historic ship that there lay buried, the weekend scavenger destroys far more than he gains.

A diver prepares to descend the anchor line to a wreck site.

REPORTING THE FIND

Whether a diver finds a new shipwreck or merely a unique historic artifact, he should report his find to either a local museum, a historical association or the Council of Underwater Archeology. His report should include his name and address, the name of the vessel, the location, the date found or the date the artifact was raised, the depth, water conditions and—most particularly—any different excavation techniques used. In this way, future divers can build on the knowledge being gained by today's underwater treasure hunters.

Happy Hunting!

4 Diving Beneath the Ice

CHAIN SAWS AND ice picks may not sound like diving gear, but for the inland diver, who lives in the cold, northern states, these tools make possible his entry into the underwater world during the long winter months.

When frosty air coats his lakes and quarries with a hard covering of ice, solid enough to walk on, the diver's only entrance to the beckoning water below is the hole he cuts or chops.

Why would anyone want to venture beneath that cold, impermeable layer? Primarily, because ice diving is the only way the northern landlocked diver can keep his "gills" wet during the cold season. The only alternative is to pack his gear away until the spring thaw and mournfully nurse an envy of his southern counterparts.

But, in addition to providing the basic necessity of water in which to dive, ice diving does offer some rewards and benefits to the brave soul willing to leave his warm living room and dare the cold. The dense algae growth that turns many of his favorite lakes to pea soup in August and September, flourishes only in warm water. Because of this, the cold water under the ice is usually extremely clear, often with better visibility than at any other time of the year.

Because of the surface layer of ice, the wind cannot affect visibility by riling up the water and scattering bottom silt, nor will rain or snow have any effect on the water conditions, other than varying the amount of sunlight.

The summertime hazard of the speed-boater is also removed. No matter how fast a snowmobiler or ice-boater zooms across the lake, he can't kick up silt. He is also not quite as likely to lop the head off an ascending diver.

The fishwatcher will be delighted to learn that the fish are much more sluggish in the cold water, many of them even in a hibernating state. That makes an ice dive an excellent occasion for studying fish or for fish photography.

Ice diving actually began—in a quarry in Wisconsin—as an adventure, one more challenge, one more environment to conquer. But, since that time, more practical applications have developed as diver-explorers began to conduct submarine studies under the Arctic and Antarctic ice.

In one exciting under-ice adventure, Dr. Carleton Ray and Michael DeCamp dove with and observed the Wendell seal beneath the six-foot-thick Antarctic crust. During their month-long stay at Turtle Rock, seven miles northeast of the U.S. McMurdo Station, they made 27 dives and spent 23-1/2 hours under the ice with some single dives lasting as long as 70 minutes.

WHO SHOULD ICE DIVE?

When under the ice, a diver cannot simply make a free ascent if he gets in trouble. A panicky swim to the surface would just result in a nasty bump on his head upon hitting the underside of the ice.

Therefore, because it is a tricky and dangerous type of diving, ice diving should not be attempted by anyone who has less than 20 hours of open water experience.

The other criteria is that the person must really want to make an ice dive. Groups should not build ice diving into an ego trip, or a method of proving oneself as a "real diver." A diver in Ohio nearly lost his life because he feared that his fellow club members would think he was "chicken" if he never took part in an ice dive.

WHERE TO DIVE

Ice diving can be done in any quarry, lake or flooded strip mine which ices over in the winter. It is best to choose a lake or an area of the lake that is about 30 to 45 feet deep at the maximum. In very deep lakes, the diver will need long lines which can become too cumbersome and unwieldy. In addition, long decompression stops in 35-degree water result in very blue divers.

It is preferable to choose a familiar body of water—one in which the diver has done open-water diving several times during the warm months. The individual will then be somewhat familiar with the underwater terrain, which may help him orient himself should he become lost.

KEEPING WARM

Ice diving is definitely a chilly hobby. Ice forms when the temperature of fresh water falls below the freezing point of 32 degrees F. The temperature of the water beneath that ice will most likely be less than 40 degrees and the air above it may be in the below-zero range.

Most people know how to keep warm in the cold air. They bundle themselves with clothes to conserve body heat. But the problem of keeping warm is compounded 25 times in water since water conducts heat 25 times faster than does air.

Statistics show that immersion in water at 40 degrees for one hour is fatal in 50% of the cases. Therefore, the first thing the ice diver must have is protection against the cold.

For extreme exposure, a dry suit can be worn. It is worn over long underwear and keeps all water out. These suits are very fragile and require constant maintenance, so they normally are not used by sport divers.

The diver who goes under the ice occasionally, most often wears a wet suit. A 3/8 inch suit will keep him warm as toast—but even a 1/4 inch suit is sufficient for most ice dives.

When exposed to the cold, the body attempts to conserve heat in the vital organs of the trunk of the body. The diver can help by wearing an extra 1/8 inch neoprene vest under his wet suit. It is surprising how much comfort that thin little vest can add.

It is important that the diver keep warm for several other reasons besides comfort. In cold water, he can lose coordination, awareness and even reasoning power if he is not properly protected. His sensations may become so numbed that he might injure himself and never realize it. Manipulative skills are cut down by the cold as it stiffens the joints of his fingers. It is even suspected that the cold diver may be more susceptible to the bends, nitrogen narcosis and other diving maladies.

A new dry-wet suit, called the Unisuit, has recently come out on the market and it is the last word in warmth and comfort. A diver who plans to do a lot of cold weather diving, should seriously consider one of these suits.

PLANNING THE DIVE

A divemaster should be chosen to guide the divers in proper ice diving procedures and to coordinate the dive. He should be someone who has been ice diving before and is thoroughly acquainted with the rules of this activity.

Before the day of the dive, he should check the qualifications of each person who wants to join the group, making sure that each one has sufficient open water experience. For those new to ice diving, he should explain the equipment needed and the rules which will be followed.

The divemaster should also plan a warm-up for after the dive. It is especially good to have a warm shelter and a hot drink nearby. A hot meal replaces lost calories, which helps build body heat, so the divemaster should check for open restaurants close to the dive site. For offering immediate warmth after the dive, a glowing fire burning on shore is terrific.

Although the celebrated St. Bernard carries a flask around his neck for reviving cold victims, alcohol does not really warm the body. In fact, tests have shown that it may even rob body heat and be harmful after exposure to the cold—sorry, friends.

AT THE SITE

After the divers have gathered at the site and been reminded of the rules of the dive and the emergency procedures, the hole must be cut. It should be near the shore, if possible, but in water deep enough for the dive. If the hole were cut in only three or four feet of water, the diver would have to slide on his belly under the ice to get to deeper water! Quarries, of course, are ideal for ice diving since often they drop straight down to 30 or 40 feet right at the waterline.

The hold must be AT LEAST four feet by five feet so that a pair of buddies can surface *together*. Time seems to go very slowly when you are hanging below the fins of your buddy waiting for him to crawl out of the hole. If you are in trouble and holding your breath, it goes even slower.

(Photo courtesy of Dudley Jones)

The hole should be large enough so that a pair of buddies can surface together.

It is best if the hole is cut large enough so that all the divers who will be down at any one time can surface together, if necessary. In the event of an emergency, the hole is the only door to their safety and if it is already full of divers when someone else below needs it, the result could be disastrous.

The best tool for cutting the hole is a chain saw. The hole should be cut in the form of a square or rectangle. The cutter must be certain to cut straight down and not slant his blade inward, or it will be impossible to submerge the block of ice, as desired. When all four sides of the block are cut and the chunk is floating free, it should be pushed underwater, then slid back under the ice. It will stick lightly to the underside of the ice and remain in place.

It is also a good idea to sprinkle some sand or gravel around the hole so that none of the divers take the plunge before they are ready. Spectators, not wearing diving gear, must be kept away from the hole or the planned fun dive may turn into a search and recovery affair.

If the ice is covered with a soft light snow, as an added safety precaution a circle should be shoveled about 100 feet around the hole. From this circle, spokes are shoveled to the hub, which is the hole. Arrows along the spokes, pointing to the hole, can also be marked. On a sunny day, this pattern can be seen clearly from the bottom and should a diver become lost he could follow the spokes to the hole.

Once the hole is ready, the divers pair up. A diver going under the ice for the first time should be buddied with a veteran ice diver if possible.

THE LIFE LINE

The single most important piece of gear in ice diving is the life line. The majority of accidents and deaths in ice diving have been the result of diving without a line. "I don't need a line. I know this lake like the back of my hand," boasts a diver—and then he never comes back.

Even in excellent visibility, it is difficult to see the hole from more than ten feet away. If silt gets kicked up, it becomes even worse. Going under the ice without a line isn't ice diving, it's attempting suicide.

Above, divers use a power auger to cut a small hole in the ice through which they can check its thickness and the depth of the water below.

The line should be strong, unfrayed rope of at least one-half inch diameter for easy handling. A yellow rope is preferred since it is highly visible. The rope should not be too stretchy or hand signals will be confusing.

One hundred feet is a good length for the line—measured from where it enters the hole. With much more than 100 or 150 feet of line in the water, the diver will find it hard to handle and easy to snarl.

A line tender handles the line from the surface, but lest he drop the line or it gets pulled from his hands, one end must be securely tied to something, like a tree on the shore.

Sometimes the diving site is too far from the shore to allow securing the line to a tree. In that case, if the ice is thick enough to support an automobile, one car should be driven out to the hole and the line tied to the bumper. The car is also a great place to sneak into to get out of the wind and cold.

Should the ice not be strong enough to support the car, there are other methods of securing a line out on the lake that can be used. One of them is to cut a small hole in the ice, about six inches from the diving hole. Then thread the end of the rope down through the diving hole and up through the small hole and tie it securely in a loop. Or, a plank, several feet longer than the diagonal measurement of the hole, can be laid on the ice and the end of the rope tied to the middle of the plank. Since it is too large to be pulled down into the hole, the plank will secure the rope adequately.

Although the line is secured, it must still be handled by a tender who works at the edge of the hole and keeps the line taut. He should be a diver, too, so that he can visualize what is happening below and understand the problems the divers may encounter. He should be in his wet suit and

If the hole is too far out on the ice to tie the life line to a tree, a long plank can be used, as in the photo above.

(Courtesy, Dudley Jones)

One important job of the surface tender is to make certain that floating ice chunks don't drift in and block the exit hole.

have his gear handy. There should also be one or two other divers suited up and ready to begin emergency procedures if someone is lost.

The tender communicates with the divers below through line signals. Any pre-arranged signals are acceptable as long as the tender and all the divers know them.

The U.S. Navy has developed some standard line-pull signals that they require all their divers to memorize. These are good signals to use since they are widely known and accepted.

Some of these signals that might be used on an ice dive can be found in the table below:

	From Tender	From Diver
1 pull	Are you all right?	I'm OK
2 pulls	Go down	Give me more line
3 pulls	Get ready to come up	Take up my slack
4 pulls	Come up	I'm coming up— pull in the line

Emergency signals:

2-2-2 I am fouled and need assistance

3-3-3 I am fouled but OK and can get out alone

4-4-4 Emergency, emergency, haul me up fast.

Line signals must be sharp, distinct pulls, strong enough to feel yet not so strong they they pull the diver up like a hooked fish or force the tender to take a swim. Before signaling, the tender must gather up all slack in the line. If no response comes, he must assume that there is still too much slack, that the line is fouled, or that there has been an accident.

There are two ways of using the life line, depending on the number of divers and their objectives. Divers can either go in pairs with one life line for each pair or all the divers that will be in the water at the same time can be attached to the same life line.

If the line-per-pair method is used, only one team should go down at a time—or, at the very most, two pair. Otherwise, the life lines can get hopelessly tangled in each other. Plus, a tender is needed for each life line, since tenders should never try to handle more than one line at a time.

If a large group will be diving on one line, they should be divided in half and dive in two shifts. In that way, one-half of the group will be available as a safety team at all times.

No matter how many divers are going in and how many are on each line, that life line should never be tied to their wrists. A diver has no control if he is being yanked around by his arm, plus the line inhibits the use of one hand.

Another No-no is attaching the line to a weight belt or tank strap. It is too easy to have the quick-release buckle or the snap come undone and the line be lost before the diver even misses it.

The anchorman—the first diver on the end of the line—should have the rope secured around his waist. A bowline knot is best to use since it will not tighten nor come loose from pulling. The line must be secured under all quick-release gear such as harnesses and belts. If the diver needs to ditch his gear he should not have to unfasten the line to do it.

If only one pair of buddies are on a life line, the second diver could be tied to the line in the same way as the anchorman, also around the waist. There should be about 10 feet of line between the two divers.

If several divers will be on one line, only the anchorman and the last man should be tied on. But, the divers in the middle may drop the line or be distracted by something, so they too must be attached in some way. The best way is to give each diver a short piece of line, about two feet long. He ties two large loops, one in each end of the small line, and puts his wrist through one loop, wraps the line over the main life line, and puts the other loop over the same wrist. He then holds the small line in his hand with the loops loosely around his wrist.

With this rig, the diver is not dangerously tied to the life line by his wrist, yet he is still securely attached. He has maximum mobility because he can slide his small line up and down the main life line as far as the next man in line.

The only reason that the last diver cannot use this rig is that he must hold the actual life line in order to receive and give line-pull signals.

OTHER GEAR AND PREPARATIONS

It is important to keep regulators warm, until they are actually going to be used, to prevent regulator freeze-up. This can happen in two ways. It first occurs on the surface if the diver tests his regulator by breathing on it before he enters the water, in which case the moisture from his breath freezes the valves into an open position. This would cause a constant free-flow of air. However, it is easy to correct. As soon as the regulator is immersed in ice cold water, the valves will free themselves.

The other cause of freeze-up is more difficult to solve and occurs in the water. As the pressure decreases in the second stage of the regulator and the air expands, this air becomes colder. The same law of physics that causes this makes Freon cool a refrigerator. In very cold water, the sudden cooling of the air can sometimes result in ice forming in the regulator. The diver may find himself sucking pieces of ice through the mouthpiece. But, this doesn't happen with all regulators and it certainly doesn't happen all the time. There is one regulator on the market, incidentally, with a special anti-freeze attachment for water colder than 38 degrees.

Before entering the water, the diver should be certain that he is properly weighted. There is nothing more annoying than the sound of a tank clanging against the underside of the ice, because the diver is too buoyant and keeps floating to the surface. On the other hand, if he is too heavy, he can ruin the visibility by kicking up silt, resulting in muck from the bottom rising to the underside of the ice.

Entering the water is easy. Fully suited up, with his tank on his back and his regulator in his mouth, the diver sits on the edge of the hole with his fins dangling in the water. With his left hand supporting him on the ice next to him, he turns his body so that his two hands are on the ice in front of him and he is hanging free in the water. Then he merely lets go and drops beneath the surface. All divers must be on the line, of course, before the first man goes in.

UNDER THE ICE

Just like Alice Through-The Looking-Glass, the diver enters a strange world when he slips through the hole. The color of everything is an eerie blue-green, as the sunlight is diffused by the ice. Everything seems to glow and sparkle.

(Courtesy, Dudley Jones)

A diver jumps into the hole from a sitting position, as two surface tenders look on.

The diver will feel as if he is swimming inside a teardrop or a crystal chandelier.

If he watches his bubbles, he will see them float up toward the surface and then flatten out under the ice like mercury splattering on the floor from a broken thermometer. In this unique world, the fish will be languid and seem unafraid of the invaders.

At first, the diver may not even feel the cold, since the water will be warmer than the air above on most winter days. And, the temperature of the water will be consistent from top to bottom with no shocking thermoclines. But, the longer the diver is down, the more warmth will be drawn from him and he will ultimately begin to feel cold. It is important not to stay down until overchilled. This can cause loss of sensation, loss of muscle strength, and even gasping for air.

Even if he is extremely warm-blooded and never feels the cold, the diver should not stay down until he is on reserve air. He must keep an eye on his underwater pressure gauge and end the dive before his tank capacity reaches that danger point.

When ending the dive, the last man on the rope signals the tender to pull in the slack as the group ascends. If he doesn't give this signal, the slack line will snarl on the way up.

It is easy to get out of the hole by giving a strong scissors-kick at the edge and pulling oneself up by the arms. Before running to the fire, the divers must replace the block of ice by sliding it back in place. The hole is then marked with flags or barriers for the protection of snowmobilers, skaters, and ice boaters.

EMERGENCY

The emergency procedures for an ice dive are vitally important and must be reviewed by the divemaster before anyone enters the water.

If a diver is lost, he should first drop straight to the bottom and look for the hole or the pattern that was shoveled around the hole. If he makes a 360 degree turn and the hole is not *immediately* visible, he must swim straight up to the surface and wait under the ice. Inflating his life vest

After an ice dive, the divemaster marks the hole with high barriers to warn snowmobilers, skaters and ice boaters.

partially by mouth will help him hang effortlessly up against the ice and conserve energy. Remaining motionless and calm and breathing slowly will conserve air. Although waiting seems long and futile—he must wait.

As soon as the diver's buddy realizes that he is missing, he must signal the group to surface and start the search. A safety line, at least 100 feet longer than the life line, must be ready and waiting. The standby divers secure this line and take it below. They swim in a 360 degree circle just below the ice, keeping the line taut and dragging it against the underside of the ice. With this procedure, the searching divers should come upon the lost diver, or the rope will sweep past him and he can grab it and follow it to safety.

With this method of search, it is therefore important that the lost diver go immediately to the surface or he may be moving further and further out of the path of the searching divers' rope. In case the lost diver is beyond the longer line, the searchers may want to carry a light which they can flash as an added way of locating him.

If he is not located on the first or second sweep, the team may want to cut another hole quickly and start a second search pattern. The diver might also be spotted from the surface through the ice. But if there has been a light snow which melted and then refroze, the surface will be opaque. Light will penetrate but shapes won't be seen.

A lost diver should not count on cutting or chipping his way through the ice with a diving knife, because in the water he has no leverage. It may sometimes be possible to find a small hole or gap in the ice where it joins the shoreline, but even this is rare. The diver's best chance is to wait for the safety line.

Ice diving is a rare experience, one for which it is well-worth enduring the cold. Although this chapter has enumerated the dangers of the sport, they are easily avoided. To put it simply, for safe and enjoyable ice diving, each member of the group must be well-trained, well-briefed and well-tied.

5 Fish-Watching in Fresh Water

OF THE MANY things for a diver to do in the underwater world, the one activity that captures him first—as early as his checkout dive—is fish-watching.

There are innumerable strange and wonderful sights in the freshwater lakes and quarries where so many divers begin their interest in the sport. On every dive, the animal life provides a submarine show to entertain and educate.

But, the majority of divers quickly lose interest in fish-watching and turn to other underwater activities. The primary reason for this loss of interest seems to be that the average diver doesn't really know how to watch fish, nor does he know what other life to look for in the freshwater sites he visits.

A diver will be far more absorbed in the scene around him, if he understands what he is looking at. If he surfaces after a dive, saying, "There were a lot of greenish fish down there, a couple of funny-looking things crawling on the bottom and some shells," then that diver doesn't know what he saw. Neither does one who must ask his buddy after every dive, "What was that fish that was down among the plants?"

On the other hand, the educated diver can report, "I saw several large pike and a school of bluegills. The crayfish were out of their holes and feeding." He is appreciating and understanding the freshwater world around him.

In addition to being able to identify the creatures, the diver should know their normal sizes and activities. Otherwise, even if he did happen to witness a new or rare happening, he would not recognize it as something special.

To help the freshwater diver, this chapter will offer a guide to the identification of freshwater life that inhabits lakes, quarries, flooded strip mines, ponds, rivers, springs—anywhere the inland diver might venture. In addition to the characteristics and habits of the familiar fishes, those of crustaceans, mollusks, amphibians and reptiles will also be covered.

A diver prepares to enter a clear freshwater quarry.

FISH IDENTIFICATION

The primary means of identifying fish are by color, markings and fins. The various fins have names. The *dorsal* fin is the one which stands up from the middle of the back of the fish. The *caudal* fin is its tail. The front pairs of fins just behind the head, which would correspond to arms or forefeet, are called the *pectoral* fins. The pair below or behind the pectorals are the *ventral* fins, and the unpaired fin on the bottom, back near the tail, is the *anal* fin. The only fin that propels the fish is its caudal fin. The others are used for balance and to change directions.

As a further aid to swimming, fish also have air bladders which make them buoyant. When a fish wishes to sink, it compresses this sac, and to rise, it inflates it.

All fish have gills, which allow them to extract oxygen from the water. Most of them, except smooth specimen like the catfish, are covered with scales. Over the scales is a slimy film which protects the fish from bacteria and infection.

Fish have varied eating habits. The carnivorous types prey on smaller fishes and for this purpose are equipped with teeth in both their jaws and the roofs of their mouths. The fish uses these teeth for chewing and also for holding onto its slippery victim. Some species are vegetarians and eat only aquatic plants. A few fishes eat both plant and animal matter.

As mentioned in the chapter on ice diving, winter is a very good time of year to observe fish. In cold weather, they drop to the bottom of the lake, become very sluggish and are extremely easy to approach. But, winter, summer, spring or fall, there will be fascinating fish to greet the diver.

The most common of all the freshwater fish—and one which can be found in most all lakes, ponds, and streams—is the perky, friendly, brightly-colored sunfish. The bodies of sunfish are short, rarely more than eight inches long, and are very round from the broadside view. Their dorsal, anal and caudal fins are all large and rounded.

There are many different types of sunfish, but they all prefer to live in cool, clear, still water. Sunfish make their nests in sand or gravel and when guarding their eggs they will defend them courageously—even from a huge, menacing man-fish. If the diver is being attacked by a little sunfish, he should look in the immediate area for a circular clearing in the sand, for the fish is probably nesting.

The best known of all the sunfish—and the unofficial mascot of the freshwater diver is the *bluegill*. It is an olive-green with darker green cross-bars on its sides and a distinctive coppery-red belly. It earns its name by having a gill flap or "ear" that is dark blue.

Bluegills often travel in schools and are usually found near water plants. They are a very curious fish, and the diver may find one peeking in his face mask, admiring its reflection.

A close relative of the bluegill is the *common sunfish*, also called a *pumpkinseed*. It is greenish-olive with a bluish cast to its sides and has lower fins of orange. Distinguished by a red spot on its gill flap, this fish is very abundant in lakes across the country.

Another member of the sunfish family is the *crappie*. There are two types: the white crappie and the black crappie. The white variety has a rounded profile with more of an S-shaped curve to its back than the black. It is mostly silver in color with dusky bars coming down over its sides from a blue back. The black crappie is darker, with spots rather than bars on its sides. Both have spotted fins and prefer small lakes and warm water.

Surprisingly, the King of American gamefishes, the *black bass*, belongs to the same general family as the spritely little sunfish. But equally as strange, the sunfish is one of the bass' favorite foods!

Black bass look very little like their round cousins. The bass is long and narrow and is a strong, quick fighter. It is a wary fish. The large ones will rarely come very close to a diver. The little ones will venture near, but if threatened, they can bolt away at top speed.

There are two familiar varieties of black bass, the largemouth and the smallmouth. Both are green mottled with black, but they are easily distinguished by the size of the mouth.

The *largemouth* has a mouth gape which extends well behind its eye. It prefers to live among aquatic vegetation in large lakes, and its range extends from St. Lawrence and the Great Lakes to Florida, Texas and northern Mexico.

The juvenile has a long, dark stripe on each side, running from its eye to its tail. Adults vary in size from a maximum of nine pounds in the north to the 14-pounder caught in Florida.

The smallmouth is smaller in size as well as mouth. It prefers rocky and sandy bottoms. As a juvenile, it has spots and bars rather than stripes and is darker than the large-mouth as an adult. The diver will find it only as far south as South Carolina and Arkansas.

A fish that is half-way between the true sunfishes and the black bass is the rock bass. In shape, it resembles the sunfish, but it has many more spines on its anal fin and a larger mouth. It is not as brightly colored, being greenish with dark mottling and a metallic cast to its sides. It is easily identified by its bright, red eyes. True to its name, the rock bass will usually be found peeking out from behind a rock or huddled in a crevice eying the diver.

If, while swimming along a mud bottom, the diver comes face to face with an ugly lump of a creature with horns and whiskers, it's not an underwater devil, it's probably just a catfish. Catfish belong to the lowest family of fishes. With some, they rate low because they are scavengers; to others, they rate high on the dinner table. Swimming along the bottom, they will eat anything—plants, animals, even carrion.

They are easily identified by their smooth scale-less skin and the barbels around their mouth. Catfish are sluggish and can be grabbed and held by a diver. But beware! Many types of catfish have barbs in their pectoral fins. They will use these to give a painful sting, as many fishermen have found out while trying to get them off a hook.

The most common type of catfish is the horned pout, also called a bullhead or a black catfish, depending on the locale. Its maximum length is 18 inches, while an average two-year-old would measure 7 inches. The young look like wiggly little black tadpoles and move around in large schools. The adult is a brownish color and the largest ones are found by river divers, particularly in the Mississippi River.

Catfish are much more active at night and would be best observed on a night dive. The ice diver will probably find them buried in the mud and hybernating through the winter.

One step up the ladder from the catfish is the *carp*. It is not a diver's friend because, when it eats, it digs up the bottom and turns clear, clean dive sites into muddy waters.

When it is not eating on the bottom, the diver will find the carp swimming at or near the thermocline. It can be identified by the four small barbels around its mouth, and by its scales, which are the largest of any freshwater fish.

It ranges in color from dark brown, green or yellow, all the way to a brassy gold or silver. The dime-store goldfish and the exotic, strangly-shaped Japanese goldfish are all mutants of the carp family, and often the resemblance will be seen in a golden carp.

The carp is not a native American fish. It was imported from Europe. Some naturalists have regretted bringing it in, because the fish is so prolific that it has become almost as much of a problem as the English starling. Not only can carp take over a lake by sheer numbers, but due to their rutting, they will destroy food and hiding places of other fish, thereby reducing other fish populations.

Moving on to a more appealing fish, consider the *perch*, a graceful little fish that lives in northern waters and prefers quiet lakes to running rivers. The perch has a dark olive back and golden yellow sides, with six or eight broad dark crossbars running from its back, down below the middle of the sides. Its lower fins are orange or red.

The diver will find perch to be very voracious, and they can easily be attracted by food. In fact, the author has many times had her fingertips nibbled by greedy perch. The young are found in shallow water at about the 20-foot mark, but the larger fish usually stay at 30 feet and below. In the winter, most of them go to deep water and then migrate inshore to breed in the spring.

The most streamlined of the freshwater fishes belong to the pike family. They have long, narrow bodies, straight as an arrow, with dorsal fins way back near the tail. In addition to making the fish look sleek, this shape also makes for speed. A diver wouldn't have a prayer of outswimming a pike on the run—not even a juvenile. A pike is a vicious-looking fish, having a large mouth full of teeth and an oversized jaw. They lurk among plants on the bottom of lakes and rivers, and will dart out swiftly at anything that looks edible.

The most common is the *northern pike*, a yellowish-olive fish with elongated light spots on its body and dark spots on its fins. It has been known to grow to a length of over four feet and a weight of 50 pounds.

The smallest of the pike family is the *pickerel*, measuring from one to 2-1/2 feet. The body is more greenish than the pike, but in shape they are almost identical.

The true king of the pike family is the *muskellunge*—commonly called musky. It lives in the Great Lakes area and northward into Canada, being especially abundant in the clear lake waters of northern Wisconsin.

With their huge heads and massive jaws, muskies are a truly terrifying sight to approach underwater. They have been known to grow to eight feet and weigh as much as 100 pounds. A four-foot musky, guarding a nest in a Wisconsin lake, was strong and aggressive enough to knock over a 6 foot 4 inch diver, kneeling on the bottom to photograph it. The musky is a solitary fish. The diver will usually see only one at a time—but with muskies, one is enough.

Going from the great to the small brings one to the *minnows*. A diver will often see clouds of tiny fish, no more than an inch or two long, swarming through the water. Even when they are told that the fish are minnows, many divers wrongly assume that they are the young of other species. But, minnows are a species all their own and never grow larger than a few inches.

Seen from above, a school of minnows looks very dull and drab. But the diver who can see them from the side will realize that they are actually very colorful and interestingly marked. They are long narrow fish, built for speed, and all have a dark-colored lateral line on each side. Because of their quickness, a diver could swim right through the middle of a school and never brush against one single minnow.

There are hundreds of varieties of minnows, including dace, shiners and chubs. The *red-bellied dace* is one of the most colorful of the family. It is normally olive-brown on top with silver sides and belly, and two black lines on each side. In the spring, the male's belly and chin turn a brilliant red and his fins become lemon yellow.

The most fascinating of the tiny fishes are the *darters*, not in the minnow family at all, but rather related to perches. Darters are bottom dwellers, with small narrow bodies topped by two semi-circular fan shaped dorsal fins. As their name suggests, rather than swimming smoothly, they dart from place to place.

One of the most interesting of the species for the diver to observe is the *Johnny darter*, a speckled olive-brown fish with a dark stripe. It rests on its pectoral fins, using them like arms or forelegs to hold the front of its body at an upward angle. From this strange position, it watches the activity around it with its big eyes. When frightened, rather than swim away, it will merely dart forward to another spot, propelled by the humming-bird-like motions of its nearly transparent fins.

The prettiest of the family is the *rainbow darter*. It has the same strange posture as the Johnny darter but is silver with red and blue markings, making it one of the most colorful of the little freshwater fishes.

The deep water diver who frequents cold, clear lakes may be lucky enough to see a trout. These beautiful speckled fish are often found deeper then 100 feet and rarely in lakes shallower than 40 feet. The most colorful of the species is the *rainbow trout*. It is silvery, with a greenish blue back and reddish sides.

The Midwest diver is more apt to see the *lake trout*, also called the Great Lakes trout, since it is abundant in those waters. It is the largest of all trout and has a brownish blue body covered with light speckles. Like most trout, it prefers deep water, but can often be seen coming to the surface to bask in the sun. Like a goat, it will eat almost anything, especially if it is shiny. Items found in their stomachs have included an open jackknife, tin cans, spoons, silver dollars and a watch and chain. So when diving among lake trout, the diver should keep an eye on his shiny knife and diving watch or the fish might try to have them for dinner.

The only "man eating" fish that lives in fresh water is a relative of the trout. It is a bloodthirsty South American fish called a *piranah*. The piranah has a small silvery body covered with spots. It is rarely more than a foot or a foot and a half long and is shaped somewhat like a bluegill. But there the resemblance to the friendly sunfish ends. The piranah has a blunt nose and a mouth full of razor sharp teeth. The fish travel in schools and when there is a hint of blood in the water, thousands will gather. They will attack any living thing moving in the water, stripping the flesh right down to the bone. Once they start feeding, they seem to go into a frenzy, becoming impossible to stop. There are instances on record of a man swimming or even wading in a piranah-infested river and being attacked and killed by these vile creatures before he could get back to shore. The diver would be smart to steer clear of water reputed to have piranah.

The freshwater cave diver will find an unusual variety of fish in his domain. In the dark, waterfilled limestone passageways, *cave fish* live. They are also called blindfish—as well they are. Since they live in total darkness, sight would be of no use to them, so nature has covered their eyes with a layer of skin. The diver needn't worry about having them bump into him, however, since their other senses are extremely acute, and they seem to have a built-in radar. The fish are colorless, since color would not be visible in the darkness anyway, and they range in length from two to five inches.

Another strange fish, which seems more like a snake than a fish, is the *eel*. Its scales are so small and so imbedded in the skin that its skin seems smooth. An eel has a long, brownish body with a long narrow dorsal fin that starts in the middle of the back, extends to the tail and then goes around the tip to meet an equally long anal fin. Since the eel goes to the ocean to lay its eggs, it is found in rivers and large lakes with access to the sea. It is a night creature, scavenging for food in the darkness and so is most familiar to the night diver.

THE CRUSTACEANS

Freshwater divers often bemoan the fact that they don't have the succulent lobsters that ocean divers bring home to the pot after a dive. But most all North American lakes and rivers have a cousin of the lobster—the *crayfish*. Also called crawfish or crawdads, they are the only large freshwater crustaceans. They grow to about five inches in length and look like miniature lobsters, each having a green, grey or brown hard-shelled body and a broad segmented tail. They are also equipped with eight legs, two claws and a pair of anteneae.

Crayfish live both in muddy rivers and crystal clear lakes. Like the lobster, they need a place to hide and will be found burrowed under rocks and sunken trees, in natural crevices of rocky quarries and lakes, and around pilings and dams.

Although they are small, their flesh is good to eat and a few freshwater divers gather and eat them. Some areas have laws governing their capture. In California, for example, the diver may only wear skin gear—no tanks. At Lake Tahoe, the limit is 50 per day.

Crayfish are fun to watch underwater. They swim backwards, undulating their tails for propulsion and trailing their claws out in front of them. The diver should remember, however, if he tries to take one out of its hole and tease it into swimming, their little claws can give him a good, healthy nip.

The cave diver will find crayfish in caverns, too, and like the fish in the deeper recesses, the crayfish are blind and colorless.

MOLLUSKS

Freshwater mollusks include clams, snails, limpets and mussels. There is a separate chapter on collecting their shells and those of their saltwater cousins, but these creatures are also interesting to observe alive in their native environments.

The *clam* is the most abundant freshwater mollusk and probably the most familiar to divers. It is a bi-valve, meaning that there are two halves to its shell. Clams commonly range in size from about a five-inch diameter to the tiny pill clams and fingernail clams which may be only 3/16 of an inch at full growth. In various sizes they may be found on sandy bottoms and among aquatic vegetation.

It is fascinating to watch them, half buried in the sand with the open end of their shell exposed. To eat, they suck in water and strain it through little fibers at the opening. But touch one and the shell quickly snaps shut. Most of the freshwater clams are not considered edible, but the fish love them. A diver will often break one open with his knife and feed it to the fish.

Mussels are very similar in size and shape to clams.

Their meat is also worthless, used only as hog feed, and is not delicious like the saltwater mussel. Most young mussels attach themselves to the fins, skin or gills of fish and are carried until they grow and drop off. This helps to spread the mussel population.

Mussel shells are used in button-making and often they secrete pearls. But the diver shouldn't plan on getting rich quick, since plastics have taken over the button industry, and it takes about a ton of mussels to produce one ounce of pearls. The pearls are of inferior quality for the most part, although some have been valued at as much as $1,500.

Snails are univalves, having one shell that grows in spirals. The larger ones will be found crawling across the sandy bottom or on rocks. Little ones like the greenish snail and the tadpole snail, or the young of the larger ones, cling to aquatic plants. Like the clams, snails will zip into their shells and slam the door behind them, if picked up by a diver.

Limpets look like half of a mussel shell, but they are actually a flattened out snail. They are usually fastened to plants, rocks or old dead shells.

AMPHIBIANS

Amphibians are smooth-skinned creatures that have neither hair nor feathers nor scales. Some live out their entire lives in the water. Others are born in the water and return to it from time to time during their adult life.

The "puppy dog" of the freshwater world is an amphibian. It is a lizardlike creature called a *salamander.* Some salamanders live on land, but there are two aquatic types which divers often see, the mud puppy and the newt.

The mud puppy has a flat head and body, with a compressed tail. It is usually about a foot long and mottled brown or grayish-brown in color. Its distinctive feature is its external gills. They are bright red and in bushy tufts just behind the jaws. Mud puppies are playful and are often handled and played with by divers.

Its smaller cousin is the spotted newt, which lives mostly in the eastern states. It has a greenish or reddish body, usually about 3-1/2 inches long, and a yellow belly with small black spots. The newt is born in the water, then spends about a year on land, and finally returns to live the rest of its life in the water.

Also in the amphibian family are the *frogs*. Divers will rarely encounter adult frogs underwater, but they will come upon schools of their young—called tadpoles or polliwogs—particularly in the late spring and early summer. Tadpoles look nothing like the creature they will eventually become. They have round fat little bodies, a long compressed tail, and external gills. They swim with a little wiggle of their tail and swarm near aquatic plants which they eat by scraping plant tissue from the leaves.

Then the change begins, taking anywhere from three weeks to several years, depending on the species. First hind legs start pushing out—weak little ineffectual limbs. Next the front legs begin to appear. These four legs grow and strengthen while the tail is slowly absorbed. Lastly, the gills turn into lungs and the little frog can leave the water. If the diver spaces his visits to a nearby lake he can watch this amazing metamorphosis of the tadpole.

REPTILES

The reptile family has the most foul-tempered and dangerous creatures that will be found in North American fresh waters—the water snakes. Sometimes these quick, slithery creatures undulating through the water decide that they don't want their privacy invaded by a diver. The *common water snake* can deliver a nasty bite with its long teeth, but its bite is not serious.

The dangerous one is its southern cousin, the *water moccasin*. Its bite is extremely poisonous and sometimes even fatal. Both snakes look the same when swimming. They average about three feet long, with a heavy, light-colored body marked with dark bands and sploches. The main differences are that the water snake's head is longer and its eyes are rounder, plus the moccasin has a prominent pit between the eyes and the nostrils.

Both snakes prefer muddy, even swampy bottoms and will be found curled up in aquatic vegetation. Or a diver may encounter one swimming mid-stream in search of a frog, salamander, fish or other creature for dinner.

The other vicious reptile is the *snapping turtle*, the

largest of the freshwater turtles. It has powerful jaws and is as ill-tempered as the water snake. Snapping turtles have been known to get as big as three feet long. The head of the turtle ends in a keen-edge, beaklike mouth, strong enough to amputate a finger or even a hand. Its shell has sharp ridges toward the tail, which is also rough and ridged.

The turtle is an air breather, but it can remain underwater for very long periods of time. It will often swim up to the surface and pull a duck under to eat it, since the turtle can eat only underwater.

LOCATING AND ATTRACTING FRESHWATER LIFE

When visiting a new lake, river or other freshwater spot, it is best to talk with some local divers or even local fishermen to find out what fish are known to be inhabitants.

Then, since most creatures like some sort of home or hiding place, the fish-watcher should head for natural habitats like sunken trees and grassy patches. Also sunken

Diver swims over an ore car at the bottom of a flooded quarry. Fish often make their homes in and around such objects.

automobiles quickly become habitats for fish and other aquatic life. In a flooded quarry that was hastily abandoned, the diver will find fish congregating around cranes, locomotives and other equipment.

Most of the fish can be attracted by feeding. The diver can bring bits of bread or meat down with him, or he can break open a clam. For especially wary fish, he may have to coax them gently, by tossing a few pieces out in front of him. Gradually he should be able to get them actually eating out of his hand.

6

Sightseeing in the Ocean

THE FRESHWATER FISH-WATCHER has much to see on a dive, but these sights are nothing compared to what awaits the ocean diver. The fish are more exotic and, particularly in reef areas, are far more colorful than freshwater varieties. There is more of an assortment in the sea and, of course, there is far more ocean to explore than there are lakes or quarries.

Besides having different animal and plant life, the sea also presents a very different diving environment. First—and most obviously—salt is added to the water. The freshwater diver who has been used to swallowing the little residue of water left after he clears his snorkle, will notice the salt, most unpleasantly, the first time he takes a good swallow. The ocean also has swells and strong currents that are far more treacherous than those found in even the largest of lakes.

The difference in environment does have its plus side, too. The visibility in the ocean is usually better and the temperature at depth is fairly constant year-round. Plus, the ocean offers mountains, valleys, and towering reefs to explore.

Where to find ocean diving is certainly no big problem since the sea covers about three-fourths of the earth. Those lucky divers who live on the East, West or Gulf Coasts of the U.S. can enjoy an ocean dive anytime they want to. The southern coastal diver is especially fortunate since he is also blessed with *warm* ocean water.

Inland divers, too, can enjoy the ocean by spending their vacations at the seashore. And more and more of them are doing just that. A Midwest scuba instructor recently stated that 90% of his students made ocean dives within one year of their certification.

Coastal residents also travel, in great numbers, to the Carribean, Bermuda and the Bahamas to enjoy the warm water and fabulous reef life. Pan American Airlines flies divers to most of these islands from New York, Miami and other cities, and all of these diving paradises are only a few hours away by air. Nassau is only 45 minutes from Miami, for example, and even far off Curacao is only 6 hours from New York City via a direct Pan Am Jet Clipper flight.

THE SEA'S CAMOUFLAGE

Plants, mammals, fish, mollusks—all types of creatures live in the sea. Although the marine world is beautiful and seems quiet and peaceful, it is a hostile world in which the strong and the large dominate the weak and the small. Not only do they dominate them—they also eat them. The ocean's feeding plan, called the food chain, operates so that most every creature has at least one mortal enemy. But, nature helps these creatures avoid their hungry cousins and keep up the population of their own species by camouflaging them in various ways. This camouflage is a large part of the fascination of the ocean's inhabitants.

The first thing most divers notice in the tropics is the bright, beautiful colors of the reef fish. Surprisingly enough, rather than attracting attention, these bright markings are often protection for the little fish. Zig-zagging colors like on the grouper, or stripes such as those which mark the spadefish, break up the definitive outline of the fish, making it less likely that a predator will notice it. Fish also assume the colors of the background or bottom so that they blend in with the scenery.

Other fish go to greater extremes to avoid their enemies. The four-eyed butterfly fish has developed an effective disguise. Predators often aim for the eye of a moving fish, so the butterfly fish sports a large black circle, which looks like an eye, on each side near its tail. Its real eyes are concealed by stripes. When a feeding fish strikes at the false eye, all it gets is a mouthful of water as the butterfly fish streaks away in the opposite direction.

The trumpet-fish is an odd-looking creature, very long and very thin with tiny hummingbird-like fins. Its strange shape is its protection. It looks just like a gorgonian sea whip. To take best advantage of this resemblance, the trumpet-fish often swims, nose down, in among the branches of soft coral, and at a glance, even a very sharp-eyed diver might not spot it.

The arrow crab, which looks like a daddy-long-legs, can easily get lost against the intricate background of the coral

The trumpetfish's method of camouflage is to swim among the gorgonian sea whips, which it resembles in shape and color. Below, one of these strange-looking creatures swims out of a clump of gorgonian coral, pictured at right.

A sight-seeing ocean diver stops to examine a clump of gorgonian coral. At its base, a spindly-legged arrow crab can barely be seen. Another one hangs half-way up a branch. The thinness of these animals is their camouflage.

reef. Its tiny body and very thin legs will particularly not be noticed among clumps of soft coral.

The sargassum fish mimics the weed in which it lives. This creature is covered with feathery filaments and loose flaps of skin, making it look exactly like the tangled sargassum weed. Even its color is a duplicate of the seaweed.

The octopus carries its own instant camouflage material. When threatened, it squirts black ink into the water around it, and while the predator stumbles around in the sudden darkness, the octopus swims away. This eight-legged creature can also change its body color to blend in with the background.

HABITS OF MARINE ANIMALS

Not only are the shapes and colors of the sea creatures interesting to watch, their habits are also absorbing. A diver could easily breathe through a whole tank, sitting in one spot and observing the strange goings-on in that one small area, without getting bored.

One of the shyest little creatures of the reef is the tube worm. It looks like a feathery tree or a futuristic flower growing out of the coral. But swim up to it, attempting to touch it, and—zip—it disappears. The feathery tentacles contract and it retreats completely into its tube which is buried in the coral. If the diver is patient and waits quietly without moving, in a few minutes, he will see the little creature "bloom" again. It is like watching a time-lapsed movie of a flower growing.

The eating habits of the parrot-fish are unique and, in an odd way, help to produce the clean, white coral sand. The fish has a hard beak with which it breaks off small chunks of coral. Its digestive system absorbs the food value from the polyps in the coral. The limestone skeleton has no food value so it is merely ground up and the fish excretes it. It is not unusual for a diver to see a feeding parrot-fish swimming along, leaving a trail of coral sand behind it.

The damselfish has a very strange bedfellow. It chooses to live in among the deadly tentacles of the sea anemone. To other fish, contact with these tentacles means death, but the damselfish is immune. So it hides in among these tentacles and pays for its protection by luring other fish into the anemone's reach. This plucky little fish is also a fearless fighter when guarding its territory. It has even attacked huge divers for invading its private coral head. But, aggressive motions from an inch-long fish don't really shake-up many divers.

A fish that's really a mouthful when it is frightened is the puffer fish. Its defense mechanism is to gulp water until it blows up like a big balloon and is too large for its adversary to swallow. One of the puffer family, called the porcupine fish, also has sharp spines. They lie flat when the fish is calm, but stick straight up when it inflates. No predator would be hungry enough to want to bite into this pin cushion.

Angelfish are pretty, friendly fish. They must be very insecure, however, because the diver will notice that their peculiarity is that they rarely swim alone, preferring to travel in pairs.

Then there is the lopsided flounder, who swims on its

side all of its adult life. It starts out swimming in the normal position when young, with an eye on each side of its head as is usual. But gradually, as it matures, one eye migrates over the top of its head and ends up on the same side as the other one. Then the fish begins swimming on its side, with the eyeless side down. To hide, it will lie flat on the bottom, sometimes digging down in the sand, its color blending in, with only its roving eyes sticking up.

The sea has a professional hitchhiker called the remora. If a diver feels a strange suction on his body and looks down to see a dark-colored smooth fish firmly attached by the top of its head, he needn't worry that he is being eaten. The remora only wants a free ride. It will often be seen attached to sharks, groupers, and other large fish, by the suction cup on the top of its head. Surprisingly, the carrier fish don't seem to mind the remora—or else they don't even feel it.

Other fish give free service rather than taking it. One of these is the cleaner fish—usually a member of the wrasse family. This tiny fish will swim around the body of a larger fish, ridding it of parasites from the skin, gill slits, and any open wounds. A fish that would normally swallow a creature of this size, will patiently hover in the water while the cleaner does its job. As mean a beast as the moray eel will even open its mouth and let the cleaner work inside its jaws—and come back out again. These little fish never seem to be in need of customers. The large fish have been known to literally line up and wait for service!

Starfish are deceptive, looking like five-pointed paper-mache stars, which lie perfectly still on the bottom of the sea. But if a diver looks closer, he will see that the starfish are very much alive and are creeping slowly across the ocean floor. If he flips one over, he will see that it moves using hundreds of tiny little tube feet. Each foot has a suction cup which allows the starfish to crawl vertically, or in any other position.

Lay one on its back, and it really puts on a show righting itself. It is also fascinating to watch one eat. It holds its victim with the tube feet, then throws part of its stomach out of its body and enfolds the food in the stomach. The digestive juices break down the food and the satiated starfish pulls its stomach back in.

One of the huge but harmless sea creatures is the manta ray. This giant ray can have a wing spread of up to 20 feet and has been known to weigh as much as 3500 pounds. They are beautiful to watch underwater, since they swim by flapping their wings. Rather than swimming, they look like they are flying. These huge rays are not to be feared by man since they eat only microscopic plankton. They could only hurt a boater or diver by bumping into him.

DANGEROUS MARINE ANIMALS

There are creatures in the sea that the diver must do more than watch—he must also watch out for them. These are creatures which will bite, sting or shock a diver; some causing only mild irritation and others causing death. Some of them are harmless as long as the diver doesn't touch them, while others may pursue and attack the diver with no apparent provocation.

The most feared creature of the sea, especially by people who have never been in the ocean, is the *shark*. It is the villain in most every underwater story, but much of its adverse notoriety is undeserved.

There are about 350 known species of sharks and only a couple dozen types have attacked man. Most divers who have spent considerable time in the ocean have been in the water with sharks who were not aggressive. More often then not, the shark will try to avoid the divers. This is not to say, however, that the threat of the shark should be totally disregarded by the diver.

A shark is a dangerous and unpredictable creature. The more voracious species include the Great White, the Mako, the Tiger, the White Tipped and the Hammerhead sharks. Nurse sharks and sand sharks have a reputation of being relatively docile bottom feeders. But even they can become vicious. There is a case of a Miami diver who pulled the tail of a peaceful nurse shark. The creature turned suddenly and sunk its teeth into his thigh. Luckily, the diver's buddies were able to free the leg and get him away from the angry shark.

Sharks have a highly developed sense of smell, plus a lateral line system that is extremely sensitive to vibrations in the water. Even from miles away a shark can sense a floundering, wounded fish. This is why a diver is more vulnerable swimming awkwardly on the surface, than he is moving smoothly through the underwater world.

Blood in the water seems to attract a shark even quicker than a floundering fish. Once sharks begin eating and the water is filled with blood, they will usually go into a feeding frenzy, biting at anything and everything. It is terribly dangerous to be in the water during such a feeding frenzy, since there is no way to stop a blood-maddened shark.

To avoid shark attack, the diver should never keep speared fish in the water with him. They should be taken immediately to the boat. If a shark is sighted, the movements of the diver must become slow, smooth and purposeful. Wild, panicky swimming will excite the shark to attack. The shark will normally be sighted first at the perifery of the diver's vision. When moving in for the kill, it swims in ever tightening circles. If this happens, the diver must keep the shark in sight, never turning his back on it. An attacking shark can sometimes be deterred by a sharp rap on the nose with a camera, a shark billy or whatever is at hand. The best weapon would be a shark dart or powerhead.

Although it looked good when Lloyd Bridges did it, stabbing a shark with a knife is a waste of energy. First of all, the shark is covered with rough, sharp denticles which are almost impossible to pierce with a knife. But even if the shark is stabbed in the tender belly, this will not stop its attack. Sharks have been brought up into a boat, gutted, and have still tried to attack several hours later.

The worst time to encounter sharks is at night, since they are night feeders. It is also unwise to dive in shark-infested waters that are muddy, with visibility almost nil.

When a shark bites, it rips and tears the flesh. Plus, it will normally come back for seconds. Death may result from hemorrhage and shock. The victim must be kept warm and gauze pressure bandages applied to stop the bleeding, while he is being rushed to a hospital.

In reputation, ocean enemy number two is the *great barracuda*. It has a long, streamlined silver body that moves like a bullet through the water. It may attain a length of six to eight feet and a good part of that length is made up of its huge mouth filled with sharp canine teeth.

These teeth are constantly on display, since the barracuda swims opening and closing its huge mouth. The fish does this only to force water over its gills, but it still is a frightening sight. When the 'cuda starts grinding its teeth (a sound quite audible underwater), that is when the diver should begin to worry.

Normally the barracuda will not attack unless it is provoked or wounded, but it is a very curious fish and may sometimes follow a diver throughout an entire dive. They are attracted to shiny objects and may bite a diver by mistake after being attracted to a bright diving watch or knife handle. They have also been known to strike at fish on a spear. If that happens, the diver should be generous and give up his dinner to the hungry 'cuda.

A barracuda's bite is quick and clean. It will normally only bite once. The wound should be treated the same as the shark's bite.

Another dangerous fellow is the *moray eel,* who lives in sub-tropical and tropical waters. It is different from the shark and barracuda in that it will not pursue the diver and will normally not attack unless he is provoked. During the day, morays hide in crevices and holes in the coral. If the diver should put his hand into a hole occupied by a moray, the eel would usually attack to defend its home. A moray bite is very serious because the eel has strong, crushing teeth and a vise-like grip. Once it has sunk its teeth into the diver, it will often hold on until it is killed—and in a few cases, even afterwards.

The great barracuda is one of the most feared fish of the ocean. Its bullet-shape makes it very fast in the water, and its large mouth has vicious canine teeth.

On a night dive, the diver might see them swimming through the water to feed. At that time, they are more dangerous and he should stay out of their way.

Similar in shape to the eel is the dread *sea snake*. Most of them are highly venomous, some having poison 50 times as potent as the king cobra's. They are found almost exclusively in the tropical Pacific and Indian Oceans, and even there are not likely to attack unprovoked. The recorded attacks have mostly occurred at river mouths and around piers and pilings where divers were working and disturbed the snakes. A bitten diver should be given emergency snakebite treatment and rushed to a hospital. It sometimes helps the treatment if the snake can be captured and brought along—dead or alive.

There are other creatures considered dangerous that will never come after a diver. Damage is done when the diver runs into them—usually by accident.

One of these is the *jellyfish*. It can't chase the diver since it has a poor means of mobility. It merely floats with the currents, or some species can move by pumping at a snail's pace through the water. The danger comes from the species that have stinging tentacles which hang down from their bodies. A wound from these tentacles may range from causing a slight skin irritation to paralysis and even death.

The most dangerous of the jellyfish is the Portugese Man-O'-War. It has a blue and pink colored air-bladder which floats on the surface and tentacles which may trail as deep as 30 feet. If a diver must surface near these, he should use his snorkle or whatever he is carrying to push them away from his body and avoid contact if possible. For some people, jellyfish stings have a cumulative effect, and a second attack would be far more serious than the first.

For a superficial wound, alchohol or a soothing lotion may be enough to ease the pain. In severe cases, hospitalization may be necessary with morphine for pain, intravenous injections of calcium gluconate for muscular spasms, and respiratory or cardiac stimulants needed.

Most every diver who has spent any time in tropical waters has been "attacked" by those devilish little pin cushions called *sea urchins*. Sea urchins are soft, fleshy little creatures covered by a round, hard shell or test.

At left is a sea urchin as it looks alive, covered with short, little sharp spines. The test, or shell, of the urchin is pictured on the right. The animal's soft body hides inside this test and the spines are attached to the outside.

Protruding from the test are sharp spines. If a diver steps on one or moves against it, these needles will pierce his skin and usually break off flush with the skin surface. They are impossible to remove, but will dissolve in a few days. If treated with antiseptic, they will normally cause no infection or bad aftereffects.

Urchins lurk in crevices and among coral outcroppings. Most "attacks" happen when a diver puts his hand into a hole without looking, or settles down on the bottom and ends up kneeling or lying on one. Divers have even backed into and sat on them and as a result spent a day or two standing up!

Another passive creature, much maligned, is the *sting ray*. It carries a stinger in a sheath at the base of its tail. The only way it can use this stinger is to fling its tail upward. If the diver should step down on the back of a sting ray, he could get stung in the ankle, but as long as he swims and watches where he is walking, the sting ray will not harm him. In fact, many divers have taken rides by holding onto the tail of a giant sting ray and being pulled.

There are several dangerous fish that have venemous spines in their dorsal fin, like the zebra fish, the lionfish and a fish called a stone fish, that looks like a clump of mud lying on the bottom. The only way one of them can hurt a diver is if he attempts to touch or grab it. If a diver is not sure what a fish is, he should never touch it. In some cases the poison of these fishes can be fatal.

Other animals like dangerous coral and shell will be covered in their own chapters.

HOW TO GET TO THE SEA

The diver can always enter the water right from the beach, but often the best reefs and diving sites are a mile or more from shore. So the diver must own, charter, or rent a dive boat. For a large boat which will hold six divers or more, sport fisherman boats, converted work boats, and headboats are excellent, because they have small cockpits and a lot of deck space.

The boat must be seaworthy, stable and equipped with a good diving ladder and/or a platform. A marine radio is a number one piece of safety equipment on a dive boat. In case of a diving accident, particularly an embolism or the bends necessitating decompression treatment, the Coast Guard can then be called immediately and helicopter pickup arranged.

Other equipment like depth finders, scanners, and Loran are handy to find shipwrecks and reefs where the water is not clear enough to see bottom. An innertube with about 200 feet of line should be floated behind the boat whenever there is a current and divers are down. Then if they surface and are carried away from the boat by the current, they can grab the line or the float, before they get too far away.

In small boats, the latest development is the inflatable boat. It can be carried in a car, assembled in minutes, launched anywhere and powered with an outboard motor. Because of its rounded pontoons, it is an extremely stable boat and almost impossible to capsize. The well-made units are strong enough to resist even sharp rocks and coral.

Jacques Cousteau used the Zodiac inflatable boat to

The inflatables make great small diving boats. Above, a 13-foot Zodiac powered by a 40 horsepower Evinrude motor, proves stable, roomy and powerful enough to take three divers, with gear, out to a shipwreck in the choppy Atlantic off the coast of New Jersey.

chase whales for his recent study and his resulting film and book. He stated that he found it faster and more maneuverable than a rigid hull.

When using a small boat like a Zodiac, it is doubly important to have radio contact with the shore. ITT Decca Marine has an excellent marine radio which can either operate on batteries in a small boat or be mounted in a larger craft using a booster bracket to supply more power. This Decca radio could be carried in the Zodiac's waterproof pouch.

The inflatable boat is also an excellent dingy or safety boat. Carried aboard a large dive boat, it will often come in handy to assist and even rescue tired divers, or it can be used to carry divers to reefs in water too shallow for the large boat.

Whether the dive boat is large or small, it should always have a diver's flag flying when there are divers down. It is equally important that the flag not be flown to and from the dive site.

LOBSTERING

Some divers just absolutely cannot look without touching, others like to bring something home to the dinner

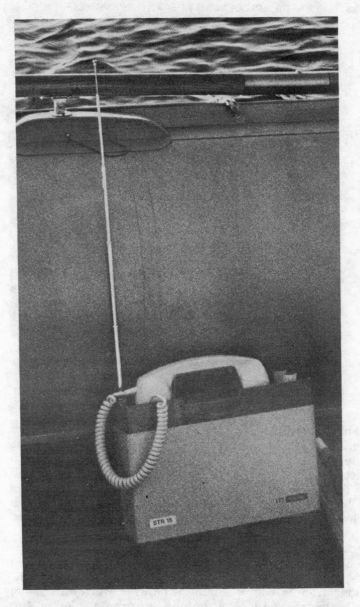

A marine radio is a must for a dive boat of any kind. Above is the portable model made by ITT Decca Marine.

Another use for a Zodiac is as a rescue boat kept aboard or tied to the larger dive boat. While it would be difficult for the dive boat to weigh anchor and go after a tired diver, the Zodiac can be quickly taken out to get him.

table and still others just plain love the taste of fresh lobster. For all these divers, gathering lobsters—or bugs as the veterans call them—is the greatest pastime in the ocean.

There are two different kinds of lobsters: the spiny lobster or Langusta, which lives in warm waters and has no claws, and the North American lobster which flourishes in the colder water and is equipped with two heavy claws—one that crushes and another that shreds.

The claws of the norther lobster make it more difficult to capture, but the delicious claw meat is worth the additional trouble. Gloves should certainly be worn when going after the clawed lobster, but they are also needed for the spiny lobster, which has a horny, sharp shell which can be very abrasive.

Spearing lobsters is not permitted in most areas, but a lobster hook may be used to induce them out of deep holes. The hook is not used to actually pull the lobster out. It is just inserted in the hole and used to "tickle" its tail forcing it to move out forward.

Lobsters will be found usually in or under something, with their antanae extended. The diver will often spot the claws of the northern type. The diver should never try to pull the lobster out by its antenae or by a leg because they are fragile and will simply break off. It should be grabbed under the body, if possible. In the case of the clawed

A diver displays the lobster he has captured. Note that its claws are banded so that it will not harm itself before he gets it home to the cooking pot.

lobster, both claws can be grabbed and held closed and used to pull it rapidly out of the hole. If the diver only grabs one claw, he is sure to get grabbed himself with the other one. A very large lobster could break a finger or even cut off a thumb.

As soon as the body is clear of the hole, the diver should let go of the lobster's claws and transfer his grip to the body. The lobster has a strange ability to cast off its claws, and the diver may otherwise find himself holding two claws while the delicious tail meat swims away.

The catch is best kept in a mesh "goodie" bag. With that type of bag, the diver can see the lobster and won't lose one, putting another into the bag.

Most areas have restrictions on the legal size of "keepers", measured from the eye socket to the beginning of the segmented tail. Taking females with eggs is also prohibited. These eggs can't be missed since they are bright red and are carried under the tail.

When the diver has his prize out of the water, he should rubberband its claws to keep it from harming itself and the other lobsters. The Langusta lobster diver needn't worry about that, however.

The lobster should be kept in an ice chest until cooking time—not in fresh water or it will suffocate.

7

Bring 'Em
Back Alive

EVEN THE MOST avid amateur diver is only underwater and among the fishes a few hours a week. The rest of the time he lives and works on land. But, how great it would be if he could bring his own little corner of the underwater world home with him!

Well, he can. A home aquarium can house some of the smaller creatures from his favorite dive spot, and keep them where he can enjoy watching their antics any time of day.

An aquarium also offers the diver a chance to observe the underwater inhabitants at length and leisure. He can learn much more about their habits and behavior than would be possible on all-too-short and infrequent dives. The hobby also provides a way that the diver, who doesn't want to venture under the ice, can keep in touch with the underwater world during the long winter months. He can enjoy an aquatic scene from the warmth and comfort of his living room chair.

A diver can collect specimen for an aquarium most anywhere he dives, whether it is in salt or fresh water. From both types of sites, he can bring 'em back alive.

OPEN WATER VS. PET SHOP FISH

Of course, the diver can stock his aquarium with fish that he buys at a pet shop, but, if he does, he's missing half the fun. Anyone can walk into a store and buy a fish, but, as a diver he has the chance to experience the thrill of capturing and collecting his own. Then, when his aquarium is admired, he can proudly say, "I caught them."

It's not much of a feat to catch a fish on a hook and line and, with all the high-powered spear guns used by divers, even spear fishing doesn't present much of a challenge anymore. But, chasing a specimen in and out of coral or rocks and finally outwitting and bagging it is quite a feat. Outmaneuvering a fish in its own environment, and then keeping it alive, is an accomplishment a diver can be proud of.

Another advantage of collecting his own fish is that they will be familiar species from his own locale, or an area he has actually visited. Pet shop fishes are usually collected in far off regions and shipped in. Or worse, they are domesticated creatures, born in captivity, having no feeling of the wild, as do the creatures seen on a dive.

WHERE TO COLLECT

Where the diver collects his aquarium inhabitants depends first on where he lives. The inland diver will find his specimen in lakes and flooded quarries, while the ocean diver can go to the sea. Both divers can bring back exotic fishes from the areas in which they spend their diving vacations.

The diver should collect in an area in which he feels comfortable and at home. Fish catching will take all his attention and concentration, so he should not be distracted by a new, strange area. Whatever the location, the amateur should not hunt in deep water. Fish brought up from way down may have a hard time adapting to the sudden decrease in water pressure. It is best to work in 30 feet of water or less, although successful collecting has been done by amateurs much deeper.

When collecting in a reef area, avoid staghorn and elkhorn beds. Fish will hide in the coarse branches and be difficult if not impossible to net. Even if a fish is ensnared, the net will probably be snagged and ripped open before the creature can be transferred to a container. The easiest area to work is around the edges of reefs and near single, isolated coral heads. Sponge beds are also good, and many small specimen can be found in inlets and along rocky coastlines.

The freshwater collector will find that many aquarium-sized fish hover around large objects like sunken automobiles and submerged trees. In areas like this, the fish are often in schools, making collecting even easier.

In either the fresh or saltwater environment, the best area in which to net fish is over a flat bottom. Since the wary creatures prefer the shelter of rocks or coral, they will often have to be chased out onto the sandy flats.

CATCHING THE FISH

The basic techniques for catching fish are the same for fresh or saltwater varieties. In both cases, the best size to go after falls in the one-to-five-inch range. These are small enough to thrive in the confinement of an aquarium, plus several little ones can be kept in an average-size tank.

The first piece of collecting equipment the diver needs is a net. Nets can be bought, but usually commercially-made nets have mesh that is too large for small specimen or else they are not large or strong enough. A diver can easily construct an ideal net for collecting. All he needs is a wire coat hanger, a piece of broomstick about 16 inches long, and some green or gray strong netting material.

The body of the coat hanger is stretched out and formed into a circle having approximately an eleven-inch diameter. Then the hook is straightened, leaving the twist in the neck intact. A notch is made in one end of the broomstick and the neck of the coat hanger is fitted into it. Then the hook is wound tightly around the stick. Onto this

Above is a simple collecting net made from a coat hanger, a piece of broomstick and some fine netting.

frame, a net bag 15 inches deep and 18 inches across is hand-sewn.

The first few times he uses his net, the collector will probably have a bad time, and may even come up empty-handed. But, with practice it gets easier and easier. A few hints, however, might make even the initial tries successful.

The cardinal rule of fish collecting is "have patience." Slow movements will not frighten fish nearly as badly as will a diver charging madly around the area. A diver can't outrun a fish, and the faster he swims, the faster it will flee. It is far better to approach slowly—from above, not beneath or behind—and try to place the net so that the fish will swim into it.

With some territorial fish, this is very easy to accomplish. A creature like the damselfish, will live in one small area, like the top of a small coral head. When defending its home base, it will swim in a pattern, weaving around and through the coral. If the diver takes the time to observe this action, he can anticipate where the fish will go and can place the net right in its path.

As soon as the fish feels the net around it, it will turn quickly and try to zip out. Therefore, when the diver sees that the fish is inside, he must immediately put the net down on a flat surface, ring down. This will seal the net and make escape impossible. Then, the diver should work the fish toward the closed end of the net, gathering the netting together with one hand, behind the fish, so that it ends up in the bottom of the net with the netting held closed above it.

Once a fish has felt the net, or realizes that the diver is menacing it, it will become wary and be doubly hard to capture. It is therefore best to get the specimen on the first pass, or go on to the pursuit of another fish while the first one calms down.

It is useful to carry a long thin pole, metal rod or other probe. A fish in a deep hole can be coaxed out with the probe and even urged right into an awaiting net.

Fish can also be tempted close to or even into a net, by using food as the enticer. In the ocean, a diver can break open a sea urchin, while in a lake, a clam will serve as food. Or, the diver may want to bring bits of bread or meat down in a plastic bag.

Collecting in a school of little fish is easy. For example, on one collecting dive, freshwater catfish, each about two inches long, were spotted. There were well over a hundred of them and they swam so close together, they looked like a dark cloud. The collector was able to swoop the net through the school and, in one pass, got more specimen than needed.

On the other hand, for a particularly wary, elusive fish, the secret might be to collect at night. On a night dive, many of the fish will be asleep and some of these are such sound sleepers that they can be picked up by hand. Even those that are not asleep can be hypnotized by the diving light and netted easily.

Once a fish has been netted, it must be transferred to a container of some sort. If the diver doesn't want to surface with each specimen captured, he must carry something in which to put the fish.

One of the best and simplest containers is a "leftover-size" plastic bag (the next size larger than the sandwich bag). Several empty bags are carried and, when a fish is netted, one bag is filled with water. The fish is put in and the bag secured with a twist tie. These bags can be carried by the collector's buddy, tied to a weight belt, or dropped into a large-mesh "goodie" bag.

Glass jars tied together can also be used for holding captured fish. They should have screw tops, and must be filled with water at the surface to keep them from imploding at depth from the increased water pressure.

It is easiest to work as a buddy team. The buddy is particularly useful in the transfer of fish from net to container. Once the collector has the fish in the net, his buddy should open the bag or jar and hold it over the gathered part of the net. Then the collector can gently turn the net inside out, pushing the fish into the jar or bag.

When diving in shallow water, or snorkling, the diver might want to keep his specimen in a floating live well. He can make one out of an innertube and a wooden bushel basket. The basket is lined with a very fine plastic screen or netting and it is secured inside the innertube so that it hangs down into the water, below the floating tube, and fills with water. A lightweight nylon line is secured to the float and held by the diver who pulls the float along as he swims. If a small weight is secured to the diver's end of the line, he can set the weight on the bottom while he is catching a fish and then return to the line with his specimen without having to worry about his live well floating away.

The diver should be selective about what he collects, choosing only healthy fish. Diseased fish can be identified by ragged fins, white spots on the body, a dorsal fin that doesn't stand erect, or visible growths or parasites. If a fish is unnaturally sluggish in its own environment, it is also to be suspected of illness.

Slurp guns can damage a fish and so are not recommended. Neither are chemicals. The mortality rate of fish, collected with tranquilizers and sleeping drugs is much higher than for those netted.

COLLECTING OTHER SALTWATER CREATURES

In addition to fish, the saltwater aquarist will want to populate his tank with some of the fascinating invertebrates. Starfish are easy to collect. They move slowly along the bottom, usually right out in the sand, and can be picked up at will. Starfish are fascinating in a tank because, like snails, they will slowly crawl up the glass side of the tank, exposing their strange undersides with myriads of suction cups.

The flowery anemones make beautiful additions and their jack-in-the-box actions are interesting to watch. If they are touched or frightened, they pull in their graceful tentacles and close up tight. When the coast is clear, they will slowly "bloom" like a time-lapsed movie of a flower growing.

Anemone attach themselves to inanimate objects and rarely move. The collector must not try to pull or pry the creature from its base. This could easily kill it. It is far better to remove part of whatever it is fastened to, and later the anemone can be induced to voluntarily let go of its former base and find a new one within the tank.

Live coral can be collected by gently breaking off a piece. The piece should be broken below the line where the live coral ends and the dead foundation coral begins. Though easy to collect, coral is almost impossible to keep alive for any length of time. This is because it eats microscopic food which is difficult to provide in an aquarium. Plus, coral is extremely sensitive to changes in temperature and salinity.

Small mollusks can be picked off the bottom or discovered buried in the sand. Tiny crabs and lobsters will be found hiding in holes in the coral reef or shipwreck where the diver is collecting. Only very small lobsters and crabs should be collected since at night they will attempt to prey on fish their size or smaller.

COLLECTING FRESHWATER PLANTS AND ANIMALS

Plants add much to the decor of a freshwater aquarium, and also provide hiding places and even food for fish. It is important when collecting rooted aquatic plants to get as much of the root as possible. The root should be dug out—not pulled out. Floating plants can be gathered on the surface with a net.

Plants should be kept in water with the fish when being brought home from the dive site. If this is not possible, wet the plants thoroughly and wrap them first in moistened gauze, then in wax paper.

Freshwater clams and snails can be picked up off the

bottom. The snails will be especially welcome in the home aquarium since they keep the walls of the tank clean. Tiny crayfish may be found in some locales, normally hiding in rocky crevices. The probe can come in handy for teasing them out.

For fish gathering in fresh water, the same techniques as for saltwater collecting can be employed.

TRANSPORTING THE CATCH

As soon as the captured creatures are brought up to the boat or back to shore, they should be transferred to a plastic bucket or waste can full of water from their own environment. The collector can also use a metal bucket if he lines it with a plastic garbage bag. Portable battery-operated air pumps, which aerate the water by pumping air through small air stones, are available at most sporting goods stores. One should be placed in each bucket.

If the diver is collecting near his home and has only a few hours drive to transport his catch, he can move them in these containers with the air pumps running continuously. The containers must be covered since the nervous fish will try to jump out, and some of the other creatures, like snails and starfish, can crawl up and over the side and escape.

If the catch must be transported for a long distance or perhaps shipped by a diver collecting at a vacation site, the collector should be prepared with large, heavy plastic shipping bags. His local pet shop or a commercial aquarium can advise where to get bags of this type.

At the dive site, each bag is half-filled with native water. The fish are put in, and into the rest of the bag, pure oxygen is released. The bags are then securely tied and placed in corrugated shipping containers. When sending the containers by commercial airline, they must be plainly marked LIVE CARGO.

SETTING UP THE AQUARIUM

Before the diver goes out collecting, he must have a home prepared and waiting for the prospective occupants. Since the water needs time to filter and age, he should begin setting up the tank at least one week before his planned collecting jaunt.

The first piece of equipment to buy is the tank. If the fish to be collected will be living in fresh water, it is permissible to use the stainless steel framed glass tanks. However, if saltwater fish are to be kept, these tanks are unacceptable. No metal can come in contact with salt water or the water will become toxic. For marine aquariums, the best kind of tanks are made of all glass and are sealed at the joints with silicone adhesive. These are very good-looking and even the freshwater collector may want to house his fish in these crystal clear homes, which have no visible supports to block the view.

The size of the tank chosen depends on the space available, but the diver should not pick one smaller than 20 gallons for this type of collection. In selecting a spot for the tank, weight as well as size must be considered. A gallon of water weighs around eight pounds, so the stand and even the floor must be able to hold that weight. The larger the tank, the easier it is to maintain, so the diver should choose the maximum size that his home and budget can accommodate.

The tank must be positioned out of the direct sunlight or the algae will overrun it and the uneven heat may harm the fish. Likewise, the tank should not be placed along a cold, outside wall nor near a window where a draft will blow across it.

Even a new tank should be thoroughly washed before use, but never with a soap or detergent. The tiniest bit of soap residue left in the tank could kill all of the inhabitants. The tank can be washed with plain water if it is not very dirty. If it needs a good scrubbing, there are safe tank cleansers available at most aquarium stores and pet shops.

The tank must be equipped with a hood for several reasons. In the first place, a fish can jump and some of the other creatures can crawl up and over the side of the tank. But, a lid is equally as important as a means of keeping fumes, such as cigarette smoke and paint spray, from contaminating the water.

In the hood, lights and a reflector are normally mounted. Artificial light enhances the appearance of the tank and makes it easier to see its contents. But more important, light is vital to the life of aquarium plants, living coral, anemone, and even the fish. Since sunlight is often difficult to control, artificial lighting is much preferred.

Fluorescent tubes are better for lighting aquariums than incandescent bulbs. The tubes give off less heat and distribute the light all along the tank rather than concentrating it in one spot.

The next concern is proper aeration and filtration. In order for the fish to have enough oxygen to breathe, the water must be kept circulating. In addition, it must be filtered to remove the dirt and waste matter, not only for appearance's sake, but also to keep the water from fouling and infecting the fish.

There are two types of recommended filter systems which also provide aeration. One is called an under-gravel

Above is an under-gravel filter. Through the tall, rear hose, the water flows down under the filter. It bubbles up through the black charcoal capsule. The perforated floor sits on the bottom of the tank.

filter and consists of a perforated, raised flooring, which is placed inside on the bottom of the tank under the gravel. A pump pulls the water down through the sand, taking the debris with it. Then air and water rise through a tubing and into an activated charcoal filter which further removes noxious matter. After leaving the filter, the air bubbles up to the surface, thereby aerating the water.

The other type of filtration system consists of a container—usually of clear plastic—which hangs outside the tank. It is filled with a layer of loose charcoal, over which is placed glass wool. A pump keeps water constantly flowing from the tank into the container, through the charcoal and wool, and back into the tank. The glass wool, which traps most of the debris, must be changed periodically as it gets dirty.

In marine aquariums, filtration is particularly vital. An under-gravel filter is a must. Often an aquarist will put one of each type of filter in a saltwater tank.

After the under-gravel filters have been set up in the clean tank, the next step is to add gravel (outside filters are installed after all the water is in the tank). Although natural beach sand may look great, it is too fine to put on the bottom of a tank. Sand will pack tightly and keep the filter from working properly.

It is best to use silica gravel (also called silica sand) since it is non-toxic in both salt and fresh water. Natural gravel should be used. Colored gravel takes away the realistic look of the setting, plus, in marine tanks, the color can bleed and make the water toxic.

One or two pounds of gravel are needed per gallon capacity of the tank. About an inch and a half to two inches of the gravel should be spread across the bottom, with the back slightly deeper and sloping down to the front of the tank.

If warm-water ocean fish will be put in the tank, a heater will also be needed. Tropical fish require a water temperature between 72 and 78 degrees Fahrenheit. The temperature must remain constant, since a variation of two degrees colder than normal could kill some of the more fragile marine fishes. To attain this even heat, the heater must be automatically operated by a thermostat. It should have an output of at least 5 watts for every gallon of water. A 40-gallon tank would need a 200-watt heater.

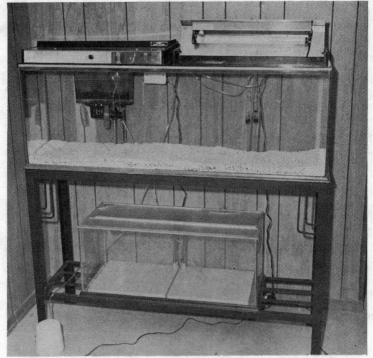

On top of the aquarium stand is a 40-gallon tank, full of water and ready for decorations and inhabitants. It has four under-gravel filters and an outside filter (at left rear of tank). The two hoods have lights and storage compartments. Below is an empty 20-gallon tank with two under-gravel filters inside.

Northern ocean fish and most freshwater fish do best in water about 68 to 70 degrees. Usually no heater is necessary to maintain that water temperature. On the contrary, the lights may need to be regulated and the water renewed with cold water to keep it from getting too warm. A floating thermometer should be kept in an unheated tank so that the coolness of the water can be checked.

DECORATING THE FRESHWATER TANK

Adding decorations, such as plants, rocks and other natural items, makes the tank much more pleasing to the eye, plus, they serve a very practical purpose. A fish needs a hiding place. Fish have actually been known to die of fright when left in a totally unadorned tank. Creatures like crayfish are used to living in or under something, and if not provided with a hiding place, they will dig up the gravel in an attempt to build a home.

Some of the rocks that are safe for freshwater use are granite, sandstone, quartz and petrified wood. Limestone rocks may dissolve in the water and increase its hardness. Sea shells and coral will also disintegrate in freshwater tanks plus, they really don't belong in a freshwater setting.

Before any rocks are placed in the tank, they must be clean. They should be thoroughly scrubbed with water and a stiff brush. Again, remember that soap and detergents are taboo for cleaning anything that goes into a fish tank.

Creative natural-looking tunnels and bridges can be constructed by gluing rocks and stones together with silicone adhesive for aquariums. The glue dries clear and will not show on the finished piece. Be sure to allow the adhesive to cure overnight before putting the creation into the tank.

Plants are essential for a natural looking freshwater aquarium. There are three types of aquatic plants: single-rooted, bunched and floating plants. Single-rooted plants are most delicate and have several stalks coming out of one root. The hardy bunched plants are so called because they are generally made up of only one long stem and must be planted in bunches to look well. Floating plants can be placed on the surface of the tank and will often act as additional fish food for the hungry inhabitants.

When a collector brings plants home, he should not put them immediately into the tank. First they must be isolated in aerated water and checked for snails and snail eggs, infestation by parasites, rotted areas, and yellow leaves. After all these things have been removed, the plants should be allowed to soak in clean water overnight and then rinsed under the tap before planting.

The plants should be put in the tank when it is about 3/4 full of water. Since fish and crustaceans are very hard on plants and will often try to uproot them, it is wise to weight them or even secure them to the bottom.

Flexible lead strips are sold in aquarium shops. These

strips can be wrapped around the cut ends or upper roots of the plants. The extra weight will keep the plants stationary. If there is an under-gravel filter in the tank, the lead strips can also be used to secure the plants to the filter floor.

Planting aquarium plants is similar to setting up a garden. A hole must be made with a finger or small stick, and the roots or the end of the cutting placed in the hole and gently covered with gravel. The crown of single-rooted plants must be left exposed.

For a well-balanced display, tall plants should be set in back and long, thin ones positioned in the rear corners. Short bunched plants look well toward the front of the tank, and one large wide plant could be used to set off the center.

DECORATING THE MARINE TANK

Plants should not be put in a marine aquarium. Most plants won't survive in salt water, and those few that will, frequently contaminate the water with harmful bacteria.

Like the freshwater aquarist, the marine collector should try to reproduce the environment from which he gathered the creatures, whether it was a coral reef or a northern shipwreck.

Hiding places for marine fish are especially important since they have been used to many cracks and crevices in their native habitats. Creatures like the anemone will also need objects on which they can fasten.

Properly cleaned and prepared shells (see chapter on shell collecting for cleaning techniques) can serve as both hiding places and foundations for sea creatures. If an empty univalve shell is placed in the tank, it is best to break a hole in the back so that water can circulate freely throughout the interior of the shell. If a pocket of water becomes trapped in a shell, it could contaminate and foul the whole tank.

Coral can be used as decorative pieces in the tank. As previously mentioned, it is very difficult to keep alive, but cleaned and bleached coral can be substituted for the living species (for preparation, see coral collecting chapter). Dyed coral is not safe in the salt water since the colors are rarely fast.

A cleaned seafan will look very graceful in a tank, particularly if it is used as a background or to camouflage filter tubes. If placed in the current made by the aeration, it will sway gracefully as it does in its natural setting.

Wood that has been in the ocean can be used in an aquarium, but it must first be soaked in fresh water for at least two weeks to kill any living organisms. There are also a few rocks that are safe for marine use, but it is wise to buy these from a marine aquarium shop.

Metal-containing rocks or metal decorations of any type must never be put in a saltwater tank. The resulting corrosion would poison the inhabitants.

WATER

Water is obviously the most important part of an aquarium. Fish not only swim in the water, they also circulate it through their gills, bringing it in direct contact with their bodies. They are, therefore, very susceptible to poisonous substances in the water.

For freshwater aquariums, tap water may be used, but not as it comes directly from the faucet. Most tap water has chlorine in it to kill bacteria. This may be healthy for the aquarist but it is fatal to his fish.

Chlorine can be removed from water by simply exposing it to air in an open container for about 24 hours. If there are no fish in the tank, as yet, the tank can be filled and the water allowed to stand. If de-chlorinated water is needed immediately, the aquarist can use one of the commercial products for this purpose. They come in tablet and liquid form and are mixed in the water to remove the chlorine in minutes.

The hardness of water is determined by the amount of dissolved minerals it holds. If his tap water is extremely hard, the aquarist must use distilled water instead. Sometimes, a half and half solution of tap water and distilled water may dilute it to the proper softness. There are kits available for measuring the hardness of aquarium water. Hardness can be estimated by checking how well soap lathers. The softer the water, the easier the soap will lather.

Another variable in water is pH. The normal reading is a

pH of 7. A smaller number means that the water has more acid, and a larger number indicates alkaline water. Tap water is normally neutral but to be sure, it can be tested with kits available at most pet shops. There are harmless chemicals available for regulating the pH of aquarium water.

When setting up a marine aquarium, all of the above variables must be checked. In addition, the water must be salt water. The diver can collect salt water from his diving spot the weekend before he makes his first collecting dive. If he does, he must carry it home in plastic or glass containers, never in metal. Then, the water must be filtered through dacron or glass wool before it is put in the tank.

It is better to collect the water from a dive boat several miles offshore since, in most cases, the water will be clearer, purer, and with less pollution than water collected near the shore.

The salinity should be checked with a device called a hydrometer, a tubular instrument which floats on the surface and measures the density of the water. If the salt content is too high, the water can be diluted with distilled water.

Some experts feel that even if ocean water is readily available, the synthetic seawater should be used. They feel that the micro-organisms contained in sea water multiply when kept in the confined space of a tank, and these can cause disease.

The seawater mix comes in crystal form and is poured into distilled or prepared tap water. Usually small packets of mineral traces are included with the salt mixture so that the resulting liquid will be similar to actual sea water. A hydrometer is necessary to gauge how much of the mixture to add.

The water goes in the tank after the gravel and decorations have been put in place. To prevent it from digging holes in the gravel and disrupting the arrangement as it is poured, a saucer should be placed on the gravel and the water poured slowly into it. Even with the saucer, the bottom will be somewhat kicked up and the water may look murky at first.

The tank must be filled right to the top or else outside filters will not work properly. Once the water is in, the outside filter, heater, thermometer, and any other equipment should be installed. Before introducing any specimens into the tank, all equipment should be turned on and allowed to operate for about a week.

INTRODUCING SPECIES TO THE TANK

After all the work of capturing a fish and bringing it home, it would be a shame to have it die as soon as it is put in its new home. This often happens however, when the impatient diver, anxious to see his prize swimming in the aquarium, dips the fish out of the bucket with a net and drops it into the tank.

An abrupt temperature change of two degrees could kill a fish, so the collector must allow the specimen to slowly adapt to its new environment. The fish should be put in a plastic bag or jar full of the water in which it was transported. The bag or jar is then floated in the aquarium until its water temperature equalizes with the rest of the tank.

When introducing a new creature to an established aquarium, this floating time also gives the old inhabitants a chance to check out the newcomer without being able to hurt it. By the time it is released, the others will usually have accepted it.

When transferring a fish, it is important that no dry object touch it. This will remove the protective layer of mucus on its skin and make it vulnerable to bacteria and fungus.

FEEDING

The new inhabitants will probably not eat the first few days they are in captivity, but the aquarist should not worry since this behavior is normal. When he begins feeding his specimens, he should start by offering live food, since this is what they are used to eating in the wild. Live brine shrimp can be bought at most aquarium shops and they will live in the refrigerator for nearly a week.

After the fish begin eating the live brine shrimp, the aquarist can switch to fresh-frozen brine shrimp. A small frozen piece should be broken off for each feeding and put in a cup with a very small amount of water. When the piece thaws, this mixture is poured into the aquarium. The light-weight shrimp will float and give the illusion of being alive.

Freshwater fish love earthworms as a treat from time to time, or tiny ground bits of heart and liver. The plant eaters will also love small pieces of lettuce.

Fish should not be overfed and, with only fish in a tank, no food should be left on the bottom after the fish have had about ten minutes to eat. But, if there are scavengers like snails or starfish in the tank, the aquarist must put in enough food so that there is some left on the bottom for them to eat.

Feeding can be used to tame specimens in the tank. The fish will soon get used to the feeding procedures and will come to the surface when a person approaches the tank. But don't be fooled into thinking that they are always hungry, since fish in confinement would overeat if fed as much as they seem to want. Lobster, crayfish and crabs can be taught to take bits of food from a hand put into their tank.

The little sea bass likes to eat frozen brine shrimp which dot the water and float like live food.

Fish can be left without food for as long as two weeks, so if the owners go on vacation, they actually don't need to worry about their aquariums. It is best, however, for periods over a week, to have someone come in and do the feeding.

TANK CARE AND MAINTENANCE

Proper maintenance and cleanliness of the tank can be a matter of life and death for the inhabitants. If anything—plant or animal—should die in the tank, it must be removed immediately. If uneaten food or waste gathers on the bottom, it must be removed with a siphoning tool. Manual and battery-operated siphons are sold at pet shops.

In saltwater aquariums, water that splashes out of the tank will evaporate and leave a salt residue. This should be cleaned immediately or the salt may start eating away exterior metal parts like the hood.

The water must be maintained. A gallon or two of fresh water with the chlorine removed should be kept on hand at all time. A little should be added as the water in the tank evaporates. In marine tanks, as the level goes down usually all that should be added is fresh water, because only the water evaporates—the salts remain in the tank. When adding water to marine aquariums, be sure to check the hydrometer.

With proper care, the captured fish and other creatures should live long and healthy lives and be a great source of pleasure to the diver and his whole family.

8 Shell Collecting
on the Bottom

OVER THE CENTURIES, very few objects have been collected
by as many people or treasured as much as shells.

Shells have had a wide variety of uses throughout the
course of history. Shell trumpets made of tritons or conchs
called the faithful to temple worship. Viking warriors used
shell drinking cups to quaff their ale. Shells were one of
the earliest forms of money, yet the cowry shell was still a
medium of exchange used in African slave trade as late as
the 19th century. Shells have also had a high place in the
fashion world since, until the age of plastics, they were cut,
shaped and polished for use as buttons.

But, besides these practical applications, the beauty of
the fragile treasures was enjoyed by many who collected
and kept shells strictly for enjoyment. Shell collections

have been found dating back to ancient Egypt and the pre-Columbian days.

The earliest recorded shell-collecting field trip was, however, not aesthetic at all. It was, in fact, a military exercise conducted by Caius Caesar in 40 A. D. He marched his Roman legions into Gaul and led them down to the sea as if to embark on an invasion of Britain. Then, at the last minute, he commanded them to collect seashells on the beach, calling their finds the "spoils of conquered ocean."

Into this age-old tradition steps the modern diver who wishes to become a shell collector, or, as the hobbyist is more formally called, a conchologist.

WHY DIVE FOR SHELLS?

Conchologists have assembled excellent collections by beach combing, wading in tide pools, searching the shoreline at low tide and never putting their head underwater. Why then should a collector turn to diving gear—or a diver decide to use his time underwater to search for shells?

Because, the diver has a distinct advantage over the collector who is high and dry. Shells picked up by the beachcomber are usually empty, the animal having died and either disintegrated or been eaten. A shell without a live occupant to keep it rooted and stable, is tossed and buffeted by the sea until it comes to rest in shallow water or on shore. By that time, the dead shell may be marred, scraped or even broken. It is usually dull since the fleshy tissues no longer protect its glossy surfaces.

The diver has the opportunity to find shells while the animals are still alive and in residence. He pursues the creatures where they live and he can choose the best specimen.

He may even discover species that never survive the rough trip to the beach and are never found by beachcombers. In addition, the diver carries his air supply with him and can therefore stay submerged long enough to dig out shells that bury themselves deeply in an attempt to escape capture.

WHAT IS A SHELL?

A shell—or seashell as the saltwater version is commonly called—is the home of an aquatic animal known as a mollusk. A mollusk is a soft-bodied, fleshy, little animal that would be utterly defenseless if it had to swim or crawl around exposed. But, kindly Mother Nature has given it the ability to manufacture a hard shell for protection.

It does this by taking lime from the water. Using a layer of tissue called the mantle to convert this material into a shell, it constructs layer upon layer as the animal grows and needs a larger house.

The shell grows as the animal matures and, in the case of mollusks like the conchs, the most mature layers are thicker and more beautifully glazed. In addition to producing the shell, the fleshy mantle protects the shiny new part of the shell from abrasions.

Each type of mollusk constructs its shell in its own way with a distinctive shape and form. There are over 100,000 different types of these shells identified and named.

The mollusks which have collectable shells can be divided into four groups: univalves, bivalves, multivalves and tooth shells.

Univalves have a single shell, usually coiled or cap-shaped, which grows in spirals of ever increasing diameters. These growth rings are called whorls. Some typical univalves are common snails and Floridian conchs.

Most univalves extend a good part of their bodies out of the shell to move and eat. They have tentacles and feelers, a well developed head, and a foot with which to crawl and dig. Fastened to the bottom of this foot is an operculum, which is a kind of trap door. When the frightened or threatened animal retreats into its shell, the operculum seals the entrance.

The second largest group of mollusks is made up of the bivalves. As the name suggests, they have a two part shell. Oysters, clams and mussels are familiar bivalves.

The two pieces—or valves—are usually identical in size and shape. They are held together by a hinge made of a strong joint or ligament. The soft animal lives between the halves of the shell, with the shell in a partially open position while the creature is eating or extending its wedgeshaped foot to move. When frightened, the bivalve

Pictured are several large univalves. Top center is a Flame Helmet Shell. Top right and left are Pink Conchs. Center is a cold water Welk. Bottom row are, left to right, a Milk Conch, a juvenile Pink Conch and a common Whelk.

retreats into the shell and uses its strong muscles to snap the halves together and hold them tightly closed.

Multivalves have a shell divided into many parts. There are not many types in this group and the most common is the chiton. Called the armadillo of the sea, the chiton has eight segments to its shell. These eight valves are held together by a leathery underskin which makes the animal the most flexible of the shelled mollusks.

The fourth group includes the tooth or tusk shells. They are round hollow tubes, open at both ends, that resemble miniature elephant tusks. Tusk shells live buried in the mud or sand and so are hard to locate. These shells live in depths as great as three miles.

Within the four main groups, there are hosts of different shells ranging from tiny limpets to the giant Indian Ocean clams that weight upto 500 pounds apiece. Because of the diversity of shells, the diver/collector should get a pictoral field guide for identifying his finds. Shells are difficult to describe, so pictures are the amateur's best aid to identification.

Pictured above, left to right, are a keyhole limpet, a cowrie, and a wentletrap.

WHERE TO DIVE FOR SHELLS

Shells can be found in all types of water, cold or warm, fresh or salt. Most any diving area, from a small quarry to the open ocean, will yield shells of some type. Shell collecting is therefore a pastime that can be enjoyed by the great majority of divers in totally diverse locations.

Each type of mollusk has its own areas and, like other aquatic life, the most colorful and intricate are found in warm, tropical salt water. In the tropics, the diver will also discover the most variety. As the water gets colder and fresher, the species get fewer and the shells get simpler in shape and less colorful.

In the United States, many of the colorful West Indian tropical shells can be found in southern Florida. The Gulf Stream side of the Keys is especially productive in late spring and summer. Also, the west coast of Florida from Tarpon Springs to Marco is favored by conchologists because of its abundance of beautiful shells.

The black and yellow periwinkles dot the coast of Maine and abundant whelks and scallops thrive south of Cape Cod. The Jersey Coast has many snail shells crawling over and around its numerous shipwrecks. Out West, California is renowned for its abalone.

The Carribean boasts Pink and Milk conchs, Helmet shells and countless other gems. The Orient and the Pacific islands have some of the rarest and most beautiful shells. The lakes and ponds of the world hold freshwater varieties of snails, limpets, mussles and clams.

Within a region, collecting areas may be further defined by the terrain. Certain types of mollusks thrive on clean sandy bottoms while others prefer rocky shorelines along inlets and jetties. Some shells live on top of shipwrecks or dead coral reefs, while others bury themselves in the mud flats. The diver/collector is offered much variety and can find intriguing specimens in nearly any water. A shell guide, or the local divers, can alert the collector to the type of mollusks he can expect to see in any area.

FINDING THE SHELLS

A novice diver may swim within a few feet of hundreds of beautiful shells on a dive and never see them. He will probably surface after the dive and emphatically declare that the area was barren.

This usually happens because he is looking for the clean, polished shells which he may have seen in a museum or display case, or he expects the shells to be laying out in the open on a sandy flat, exposing their vulnerable, colorful parts like a banner to attract the diver. If this is what he looks for, the diver will have no luck as a collector.

Like most of nature's other creatures, mollusks try to go about unnoticed and thereby in safety, so they camouflage themselves. Some, like the carrier shells, even go so far as to attach bits of old dead coral, loose stones, and broken shells to the back of their own shells, in order to disguise themselves from the hungry eyes of predators.

In univalves, the pearlescent, colorful part of the shell faces downward, and the top of the shell is nondescript to blend with the terrain. To escape detection, shells also hide in crevices of rocks and coral and bury themselves in the sand.

Snorkling over a reef at top speed, the diver will never find anything. He must move slowly and look well—under, around and on top of everything in sight.

In a saltwater environment, the first place to check is the sand around and among the coral reefs or other large objects underwater. In a lake or pond, the sand around logs, fish pens and other habitats is usually the most productive. Large shells like conchs or snails may often be seen lying right out in the open. They are, however, easy to miss since they may be the same color as the bottom or covered with a light dusting of sand. A hump in the sand may indicate that a shell is buried just beneath the surface.

If no shells are visible, the diver should look for bubbles coming up out of the sand or for a hole like one that might be dug by a miniature gopher. This may very well be the breathing hole of a buried mollusk. If the diver digs quickly, he will turn up a prize. Since the diver will usually not know ahead of time which type of shell is buried beneath the breathing inlet, he should dig carefully and to one side of the hole to avoid breaking the shell. Pen shells, for example, which frequently bury themselves, are extremely fragile and would be ruined if hit with a spade or knife.

Another telltale sign in the sand is the trail a mollusk leaves behind as it pulls itself along by its foot. If the diver follows the trail in both directions, he will probably come upon the submarine bulldozer that excavated the sandy road.

Mollusks usually do not attach themselves to live, stony coral, but they can be found attached to dead coral and to other inanimate materials like remains of ships, fish traps, and rocks. If the diver turns back the rocks or pieces of coral and debris, he will often find lovely little shells clinging to the undersides. The diver must be certain to re-place anything he turns over or he may disturb the eco-logical balance. For example, a rock not turned back, could expose newly laid mollusk eggs to the sunlight and destroy them.

One very beautiful shell, the flamingo tongue, is always found clinging to sea fans or sea whips. At a glance, it looks like a spotted caterpiller crawling up the soft coral, but this coloring is actually on its mantle. The empty shell is cu-cumber shaped, a pearlescent orangish-white, and only about an inch long. The collector can pluck these shells off the sea fans like picking apples from a tree.

Some mollusks are nocturnal and come out of hiding only at night. The night diver will discover that areas which were empty by day are crawling with hungry creatures by

A diver gets ready to descend and collect mussel shells along the rocky inlet. She carries a collecting bag and a knife to pry off the shells.

night. In the glow of his underwater light, he will see many collectable specimens.

For the tiny shells, smaller than a fingernail, the diver should take down several small jars and scoop up bottom samples from various parts of the dive site. Back on shore, he can sift the sand through a close mesh and he will often find members of the small species and juvenile shells.

After finding the shell and before bringing it up to the surface, the diver may want to observe the creature in its natural habitat. Observing can be just as fascinating as collecting. A conch crawling on the sand will slip into its shell and slam the trap door. The diver could then pop it into his collecting bag. But if he leaves it on the sand for a few minutes, he will observe how the creature cautiously ventures out and begins a slow, lumbering walk in an attempt to gain the safety of the reef. Observing the creatures adds another dimension to shell collecting because the collector then can answer questions and offer anecdotes about his specimens.

EQUIPMENT

For shell collecting, the diver does not need a lot of expensive, extra equipment besides his regular scuba gear. In fact, with practice a diver can collect on breath-holding dives wearing only mask, fins and snorkle.

There are, however, a few basic pieces of gear which can make shell collecting easier. First, the diver needs something in which to carry his prizes. A canvas or mesh "goodie bag" is fine for carrying the larger shells. A great improvised carrier is a heavy, clear plastic laundry bag.

Since there is no mesh through which the tiny shells can escape, shells of all sizes can be kept in this type of bag. Because it is transparent, the diver can see what he has during the dive.

For collecting small shells, a Jensen belt is handy and it can very readily be made at home. The device is made up of a canvas belt approximately two inches wide, fitted with open pockets of elastic canvas. Into these pockets, polyethylene screw-top bottles are inserted. The tiny shells are placed in the bottles.

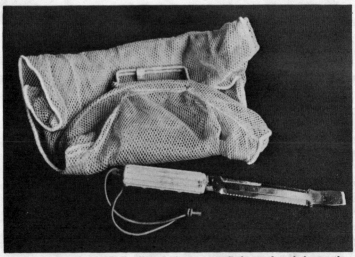

The instruments of a shell collecting diver—a goodie bag and an abalone tool.

When wearing a Jensen belt, the diver must remember to fill the bottles with water before he attempts to descend, otherwise they will act as a float, making it difficult for him to submerge. Further, if he manages to get down with the bottles empty, the pressure of the water will cause them to collapse. In other words, the diver will suffer from "bottle squeeze."

A diving knife is useful for prying up small or weak shells, but for tough ones like the abalone, a crowbar or abalone tool is needed. For some California abalone, it takes all the weight of the diver on the other end of the lever to pry up the tenacious mollusks.

A small shovel, a long narrow-bladed trowel, or a gardening fork can be carried for digging out shells which bury themselves, and a pair of tweezers can be used for getting tiny shells out of the crevices in rocks and coral. The diver might also want to carry some bait, like bits of conch or clam, to tempt carnivorous specimen out of hiding.

DANGEROUS SHELLS

There are some shells that should not be collected—or if they are collected they must be handled with extreme caution. These are the poisonous cone shells.

The fatal members of the species are usually found in tropical Pacific waters and their sting is as poisonous and deadly as a rattlesnake's bite. In severe cases, death can occur in a matter of hours.

Obviously the cone shell will not pursue a diver, but when picked up and frightened, the animal will thrust out a cluster of venom-filled teeth which puncture the skin. A victim must be rushed to a hospital immediately and emergency snakebite treatment performed on the way if possible.

CLEANING AND PRESERVING

Many beautiful shells brought home by the diver have ended up out in the trash can because the collector didn't realize that there was a decaying animal inside that needed to be—and could easily be—removed.

As soon as the diver brings his catch to shore, he should begin preparing his specimen. Several of the techniques for cleaning shells must be initiated while the animal inside is still alive.

Bivalves are the easiest of all shells to clean. If a marine shell is placed in fresh water, the creature inside will die and the shell will usually open. Then the animal can easily be cut out and disposed of. The inside of the shell should then be scraped clean with a piece of hardwood or the *back* of a knife blade. Care must be taken not to scratch or injure the interior of the shell since, in the bivalves, this is usually the pretty, glossy part of the specimen.

If the diver wants to display the bivalve with its two halves joined and in an open position, he must be careful not to cut the hinge. Then when the shell is cleaned, but still wet, it should be laid out on a flat surface with a piece of wood or other material holding the two halves open as far apart as is desired. When the shell dries, it will remain in that open position.

Univalves are far more difficult to clean than bivalves. The dying animal will retreat far back into its shell, seeming almost inaccessible. Also, since he can't see in, the diver may leave bits and pieces inside which will decay.

Boiling the mollusk is promoted as an easy way to soften the muscle of the creature and allow the collector to pull it out intact. It is, however, not the best method to use, since boiling often dulls and even ruins the shell due to the rapid temperature change. If the shell is to be boiled, all changes in temperature must be gradual. First, the shell must be placed in a pot or kettle of lukewarm water. The water is then slowly brought to a boil and the shell allowed to boil for *no more than ten minutes*. The pot must then be removed from the fire and left—with the shell still in the water—to cool naturally. Or cold water can be added a little bit at a time to bring the temperature of the water down gradually. The shell must not be removed immediately after boiling nor be immersed in already boiling water.

After the boiling process is completed the animal can be pulled out. When removing the animal—after whatever initial process is used—take a safety pin, ice pick or coat hanger to hook the animal and pull it out. Hold the hook still and turn the shell, corkscrew fashion, in the direction of the spiral whorls.

Some large mollusks, like snails, conchs and helmets, can be hung to remove the animal. The foot is either tied or hooked with a wire coat hanger and the string or wire secured so that the shell hangs free below the foot. The weight of the shell will gradually pull the animal free in a day or two. Be sure the ground beneath the shell is soft or padded because as soon as the animal is pulled free, the shell will drop.

If time permits, shells can be cleaned by burying them in soft dry sand. Either insects will eat the meat or, over a period of several weeks, the meat will rot and turn to liquid. When burying the shell, it must be laid with the opening down so that the liquid can drain out, otherwise it may stain the shell.

Freezing is another way of loosening the animal in a univalve. The problems of rapid temperature change apply to this process also, so freezing must be done gradually to avoid getting fine cracks in the enamel of glossy shells. The live mollusk is placed in a plastic bag and then put in the bottom part of the refrigerator for a few hours. It is then transferred to the freezer and left for two or three days. To thaw, place it back in the refrigerator for about 12 hours and then in a bucket or sink full of cold water for another two or three hours. When it has completely thawed, the meat should come out easily.

When cleaning his shells, the diver should keep and clean the operculum, that little round disk that acts as the mollusk's front door. For display, the operculum can be glued to a cottonball and replaced in the shell in its natural position.

Univalves, too small to be dug out, can be soaked for several days in a four percent solution of formaldehyde. Mix one part commercial formaldehyde to ten parts water. Or, a solution of 70 percent grain alcohol can be used. Divers on vacation in the Caribbean islands have found that, in addition to its more obvious uses, the strong Jamaican rum makes a successful soak for small shells. One diver poured a shot of rum in a shell inhabited by a hermit crab, who refused to leave. Within a minute or two, out came a very wobbly little fellow who zig-zagged his way, in a most un-crablike pattern, to the water—probably to sober up.

After the small shells have been soaked in a pre- servative, they need only be washed in fresh water. Al- though the meat parts will still be left inside, they will be preserved and will not give out any foul odor.

The tusk and tooth shells can be cleaned and preserved in the same manner as small univalves. Chitons and other multivalves are a bit more, difficult. As soon as it is taken out of the water, a chiton will curl up into a tight ball which is impossible to uncurl, even by force. Drop the live specimen into a pail of salt water until it straightens out. Then quickly place it on a flat, wet piece of wood and tie it securely with string. Soak the animal and the wood in fresh water for several hours to kill it. Then untie it, scrape the meat out and retie it until the shell has dried.

With all types of shells, after the animal has been removed, the outside of the shell itself must be cleaned. The non-glossy outside of shells like the conch can be scrubbed with a stiff brush and a detergent, then rinsed in clear water. Glossy shells like cowries and the enameled parts of other shells will usually need little more than a rinsing and a light buffing to bring out the shine. Brush the shell lightly and sparingly with mineral oil or baby oil to bring out the color of the shell, particularly on its non- glossy surfaces.

DISPLAYING THE SHELLS

Shells can be displayed in many ways depending on the size of the diver's collection and his tastes. Single, large shells can be placed decoratively and mixed in with other items on end tables, bookcases, room dividers and other furniture throughout the house.

Or, special display cases or shelves can be used to show the collection. It is best to place large numbers of shells like this behind glass, since they can be terrible dust catchers.

Little shells can be stored attractively in match boxes, empty typewriter-ribbon boxes, or small cardboard jewelry boxes. For display, lay the shell or shells on a cot- ton background and cover the entire container with plastic wrap.

However the shells are displayed, they should be labeled with the name of the shell, the location and date of the find, and the collector's name. If the collector does not want to attach a label with all this information to a shell on display, he can ink or glue a tiny number on the shell and then record the information in a notebook. This information will come in handy because invariably the first questions guests ask are: "What is that called?" and "Where did you get it?"

If the diver gathers a good number of small common shells, he might want to go creative. Shellcraft is becoming a popular hobby with supplies available at most do-it-yourself stores. Shells can be worked into jewelry, pictures, paperweights, little figurines—whatever the imagination can come up with.

The uses of shells are innumerable, but the diver should remember one important rule: "Collect only what you will use." If this rule is followed, there will be shells left to delight and fascinate other divers for years to come.

9 Coral Gathering

THE MOST FASCINATING animals of the sea are so tiny that they can hardly be seen, yet they are the master builders of the largest structures in the ocean, the vast rocky reefs that tower up from the depths and run for hundreds of miles.

These miraculous little animals are called coral polyps and they construct the beautiful coral reefs that make diving in the tropics such a treat.

As mentioned in the chapter on aquariums, coral can sometimes be kept alive in a marine tank so that the beautiful colors of the feathery polyps can be seen and enjoyed. But maintaining live coral for any length of time is an extremely difficult task, since the coral feeds on tiny organisms which often cannot be provided by the aquarist. Also the coral is extremely sensitive to temperature, salinity, and other water conditions.

There is another way the diver can transport the delights of the coral from the reef to his home. As the conchologist gathers the houses of shellfish to display, so the diver going after coral can accumulate a collection of the houses built by the various coral polyps.

These houses range in shape from three-foot branches that look like a deer's antlers to rotund mounds resembling a human brain. Although the color is lost in collecting coral that is no longer alive, the fantastic shapes make marvelous decorator pieces.

WHAT IS CORAL?

A piece of coral might be likened to a huge apartment building, full of one room apartments, each room having a single occupant. The strangeness in this comparison is that when an occupant dies, his room remains forever vacant. New tenants build their own rooms and attach them to the rest of the building on top of the empty rooms.

The house of the coral animal is actually his skeleton, which he wears outside instead of inside his body. A polyp has the unusual ability to take calcium salts from the sea and change them into hard calcareous rock. It uses this substance to construct a limestone cup around itself.

The animal lives its entire life in the cup, extending only its feathery tentacles to feed. These tentacles have the ability to shoot microscopic poison darts which paralyze the prey. The tentacles then turn inward and guide the food toward the mouth.

Most corals are colonies of hundreds of these tiny polyps attached to each other by their limestone cups. The live coral builds on top of dead coral and so, over hundreds and thousands of years, the gigantic mountains of coral have come to exist. Entire island chains, such as the Bermudas, have been slowly and steadily built by these creatures, and in later years were exposed to the air by the receding ocean.

The rate of growth for coral is extremely slow. It is estimated, for example, that a piece of staghorn coral will grow from 1/2 to 2 inches a year. It can grow only in depths shallower than 150 feet because it needs the strong sunlight. Also, since it is unable to move in search of its food, it

The polyps live in the tiny cups of coral they construct. On this closeup of a piece of elkhorn coral, the cups resemble enlarged pores.

must be exposed to water currents or wave action that will carry food to its waiting tentacles.

There are other members of the coral family besides the diligent reefbuilders. These are the gorgonians, also called soft corals. One of the gorgonian types is the sea whip, a brilliantly-colored colony of polyps, which looks far more like a plant than an animal as its whip-like branches wave gracefully in the current. These soft corals are not good for collecting since they don't produce limestone frames, but rather have a horny, flexible skeleton.

The sea fans are also gorgonians, but they can be collected since they can be dried and will even sometimes retain their beautiful orange and purple colors. Looking like lacy giant fans, they, too, undulate to the rhythm of the current.

One other exception in the coral family is the solitary coral. Rather than supporting a whole colony of polyps, this type has only one polyp for the entire structure. The mushroom coral is an example of a solitary coral. It is small and lives in comparatively deep water.

WHERE TO FIND CORAL

The best place to hunt for coral specimens is in the warm tropic waters which harbor the prolific coral reefs. Coral thrives in 73 to 77 degree water, so in seas which maintain these temperatures all year around, the coral will be most abundant and the greatest number of varieties will be found.

Coral reefs are abundant on the eastern coasts of North America, South America, Central America, Africa and Australia. The largest coral formation in the world is the Great Barrier Reef which extends more than 1200 miles along the eastern shores of Australia. But the western shores of these same land masses have few or no coral reefs.

Coral is not limited to the tropics and can, in fact, be found in every ocean—even the cold seas of the Arctic and Antarctic circles. A beautiful bright orange coral is abundant in the waters of New York and New Jersey. These cold water corals, however, are small. They grow in little patches and never build great reefs.

The only true coral reefs in the United States' continental waters are off the coast of southern Florida and the Florida Keys. These reefs are bank reefs and the Keys are actually made of coral. The living reefs are a mile or two offshore and go north only as far as Miami.

Although the U.S. doesn't have much in the way of coral reefs, there are many islands nearby where Americans can vacation and find exquisite coral formations. The reefs of British Honduras—in Central America, off the coast of the new republic of Belize—are second only to the Great Barrier Reef. The British Honduran reefs extend, unbroken, for over 125 miles and are the longest in the West Indies.

The islands of Bermuda, just 600 miles from the Carolinas, feature the northernmost coral reefs in the

On a coral reef, many different varieties of coral grow together. In the section of reef pictured above, star coral dominates the center, with a piece of brain coral to the right and fire coral in the foreground. One of the coral reef's inhabitants, a spiny sea urchin, peeks out from beneath the star coral.

world. Coral grows there only because of the warm water carried to the islands by the Gulf Stream, which flows past the islands all year around. Bermuda waters are the clearest in the Atlantic Ocean and in many areas the reefs are close enough to swim to from shore.

The Bahamas consist of almost 700 islands, dotting 100,000 square miles of Atlantic Ocean. The nearest island is only 60 miles east of Palm Beach, Florida. The reefs are highly developed and offer a great assortment of corals. The out islands of Abaco, Eleuthera and Andros have the best reefs along their eastern shores. The reefs of Nassau and Freeport are also excellent although not as virgin.

For those willing to travel a little farther, the Carribean islands of Jamaica, the Caymans, the Virgin Islands, and the rest of the West Indies have a great variety of coral formations.

STONY CORAL IDENTIFICATION

Since the stony or limestone-producing corals are the ones the collector is mainly interested in, some of the more common species of this type should be identified. Coral identification may sound like a momentous task, since there are some twenty-five hundred species of coral. But, a good many of these are just variations of one type of coral and have the same characteristics and the same common name.

The beginner coral collector need learn only a few of the common names and he will then recognize familiar corals no matter where he dives. Since the Latin names are used for universal recognition, that name most normally associated with each common name will be given in parenthesis.

The type most distinctive and easy to identify is the *staghorn* coral (Acropora cervicornis). As its name suggests, it is shaped like a stag's horns or a deer's antlers. Underwater it is a brownish-yellow and the little polyp cups protrude all over the surface of the "branches" of the coral. Small bunches of staghorn coral will sometimes be

Above are several types of bleached branching corals. They are (top row, left to right) finger coral, blossom coral, and staghorn coral. In the bottom row is a piece of juvenile elkhorn coral and, lower right, some leaf or lettuce coral.

found growing in among other corals on a reef. It will also be found in vast fields of nothing but staghorn coral.

This coral grows from the tip upwards, so the live coral will be on the ends while the stalk or root may be dead. Because of its delicate shape, staghorn is an excellent coral for decorative uses and is often sold in pet shops for use in aquariums.

A similar type of coral, and a relative of the staghorn, is the elkhorn coral (Acropora palmata). It, too, resembles its name, looking like elk or moose horns. The color is the same brownish yellow as the staghorn but the branches are much thicker and flatter. Elkhorn often grows in large fields in very shallow water.

A novel specimen, ideal for collecting, is called the brain coral (Meandrina meandrites). It always grows in a round boulder shape and is covered with zig-zagging valleys, resembling the convolutions of a brain. The specimen range in size from pieces smaller than a cat's brain to huge pieces bigger than a man, which would fit the cranium of a giant. The live brain coral builds an outer layer over the dead

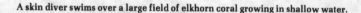

A skin diver swims over a large field of elkhorn coral growing in shallow water.

coral so that the visible part is all alive, while underneath and inside it is dead.

The *flower* coral or *blossom* coral (Eusmilia fastigiata) is one of the most beautiful corals to collect. It resembles a nosegay of flowers with bud-like blossoms. The central stalk branches out into many smaller stalks, each of which has one or two blossoms. The blossoms are the live part of the coral on this species. The base is usually brown and the blossoms greenish. The tentacles which protrude are white.

A similar species is the *tube* coral (Cladocora arbuscula). It looks like flower coral on which the buds haven't opened. Its colors are the same but its branches may be a little more dense than the flower coral.

A very pretty and delicate coral is the *leaf* or *lettuce* coral (Agricia agaricites). It looks like leaf lettuce or pieces of cabbage, and ranges in color from chocolate to purple-brown. The polyps live on and protrude from both sides of the leaves and have short white tentacles.

The *hat* coral (Agaricia fragilis) is a relative of the leaf coral and looks like one large, saucerlike leaf. The polyp's cups are only on the upper side of the leaf.

A common branching coral is the *finger* coral. It goes under the general name "Porites" and there are many varieties, depending on the length and thickness of the "fingers." They range from the porous coral (Porites astreoides) which forms rounded bumps, to the clubbed finger coral (Porites porites) which has short, stubby fingers, and all the way up to the common finger coral (Porites furcata) which has long graceful digits. Most varieties are a yellowish brown.

A piece which often finds its way to a desk as a paper-weight is called the *rose* coral (Manicina areolata). Its shape is oval with a rounded top. It grows out of a short narrow stalk underneath and is rarely over six inches long. The top of the rose coral is somewhat similar to a brain coral, but its convolutions are much higher, more prominent and more feathery looking. Its colors range from yellow to brown with a green tint in its valleys and transparent tentacles with white tips.

The most common type of coral is the *star* coral. No Latin name will be given for it since it has so very many names in

Three solid, round corals pictured below are (l. to r.) brain coral, star coral and rose coral.

all of its various forms. The common denominator which makes coral a star coral is that the polyp cup is round and flush to the surface of the skeleton. Up close it looks like an intricate snowflake. It is one of the principal reef-forming corals and can grow to become huge boulders. Its color runs the gamut from the bright orange species of New York to the kelly-green, velvety star coral so abundant in Jamaica.

Fire coral or *stinging* coral (Millepora alcicornia) is not a true coral but it grows among the reefs and is made up of polyps in a limestone skeleton. It is easy to see the difference, since, unlike true coral, it has a smooth surface. Its polyps are minute, looking like pinholes. Its shape varies but it is usually leaf-like and is a mustard color with white edging. The tentacles of fire coral are equipped with stinging cells and a diver who touches them will get a painful sting and may even get angry red welts which last for several days.

Another false coral that is very attractive is the *organpipe* coral (Tubipora musica). It takes the form of little tubes running parallel to each other and attached by little platforms. Its skeleton, when cleaned, has a deep red color, but alive the coral looks green since long green tentacles protrude from each tube.

Just as the stamp collector prizes special issues with rare postmarks above the ordinary stamps, the coral collector too, has his precious corals, more rare and more valuable than the ordinary species. One of these is *black* coral. Underwater, it looks like a reddish-black tree. When a diver brings it to the surface, he will see that it is covered with a sticky slime. Beneath this layer, the coral is hard and black. Black coral is beautiful to display in its tree-like state, or jewelry can be made from polished pieces taken from the central core of black coral that is thick enough and of high quality.

Since it is highly prized, black coral has been picked quite extensively, so, in most areas, divers must go very deep—in excess of 150 feet—to collect this coral.

The commercial *red* coral (Corallium nobile) is the species of which coral jewelry is made. Like black coral, it is soft in the water but turns hard when brought up and

This is how a patch of the dread fire coral looks underwater. Note the white edging on the leafy coral.

exposed to the air. The pieces for polishing also come from the central core. Red coral has a long history of legends attached to it and it was used for medicinal purposes until recent times.

COLLECTING CORAL

The numerous souvenir shops that sell pieces of coral worked into lamps, pen sets, ashtrays, etc. are one of the major causes of the decimation of many beautiful reefs. The problem is that many of these commercial collectors go down with dynamite and blow apart large sections of the reef. They often destroy far more than they collect.

The responsible diver-collector should never use blasting to detach his specimen. He should check first to see if there are loose, unattached pieces of the coral he wants. If not, then he can break or pry off the items he needs. But he should choose only the pieces he will use, and not tear up the reef indiscriminately.

When collecting, the diver must not be blind to the natural balance of the reef. If taking a certain piece of coral will upset several occupants of the reef or destroy a beautiful panorama, the diver should look elsewhere for hes specimen.

The reef must be protected from divers, but likewise while collecting, the divers must protect themselves from the reef, too. Most stoney corals are sharp and they can cause nasty cuts and scratches that often become infected. If the water is too warm for a wet suit, the diver should wear a pair of tight old jeans or leotards to protect his legs and some type of long-sleeved shirt.

If the diver does get coral cuts, he should clean them out with a solution of spirits of ammonia. This will sting but will keep out infection and minimize scarring.

Gloves must always be worn. The plasticized canvas work gloves are excellent for collecting coral, or for more flexibility, rubber household gloves can be worn.

Some of the branching corals, like staghorn, can be broken off by hand. Others, such as the brain corals and rose corals, are usually firmly cemented at the bottom or to old dead coral. For these, a great instrument to use is an abalone tool. It can be used to pry like a crowbar and it also has a serrated edge for sawing and cutting.

When collecting specimen for a particular purpose, the diver may have a special shape or type of coral in mind. Since the movement of the water has a lot to do with shapes of coral, the diver should look for the more massive, thick, short corals in rough water, and branching coral with thin delicate plates in calm seas. In very deep water, he will come upon spindle or pillar shapes.

CLEANING AND PRESERVING THE SPECIMEN

A piece of coral, brought out of the sea and left in the air, will soon begin to develop a bad odor, since the animals inside start dying as soon as they are out of the water. Therefore, the specimen must be cleaned and preserved if it is to become a collectable piece.

There is really no way to preserve the underwater colors of the coral, since the color comes from the living tissue of the polyps. But the intricate limestone skeleton can easily be kept.

When the coral is brought ashore, the first thing to do is scour it with a stiff brush to remove the thin layer of flesh that covers the skeleton. If the coral is fragile, this cleaning must be done gently, and a toothbrush is probably the best instrument to use.

If the diver happens to be on vacation at the shore, or lives on the ocean, he can clean and bleach the coral naturally. He must secure the pieces of coral in shallow water so that the action of the waves and surf will scrub the coral, cleaning out many of the polyps.

After about a day, the pieces should be taken out of the water and laid in the sun to dry. Alternating the water and sun treatments—a day in the surf, followed by a day in the sun, then back into the water, etc.—will result in a very clean piece of coral bleached by the sun.

For small and fragile pieces, or when the diver will not be at the shore for enough days to complete the sun and sea treatment, the best cleaning agent to use is ordinary laundry bleach. In a bucket or barrel, the collector mixes one part liquid *chlorine* bleach to approximately five parts fresh water. The coral is left in this solution until the skeleton is all white and clean. Then the piece is washed under a hard spray of water and set out to dry—in the sun if possible. If the coral is to be put in a living aquarium, it must be soaked in fresh water for at least two weeks before it can be introduced into the tank. During the treatment period, the water must be changed every day or two.

Sea fans are preserved in a different manner. They should not be placed in bleach since it will take away the color of the coral, which in this case is preservable. While the coral is still soft, the layer of marine slime should be removed with a soft brush or a damp cloth. Then the sea fan should be laid out flat on newspapers to dry—out of the direct sunlight. It is important to place the sea fan in the shape and position desired, since once it dries it becomes hard and brittle.

Black coral is another species that should not be bleached. It needs brushing and several washings in fresh water to remove the slime, and then drying in the shade.

DISPLAYING THE CORAL

There are so many decorative things that can be done with the preserved pieces of coral. A large brain coral makes an excellent doorstop. Simply glue a heavy piece of felt to the bottom of the piece to protect the floor or carpeting.

A small brain coral, a rose coral, or any other rock-like coral can be fitted with a felt bottom and used as a paperweight or merely a decorative conversation piece on a cocktail table.

Two matching pieces can be glued to a wooden base and backing and turned into an interesting set of bookends. Pieces of coral can be similarly used to decorate jewelry boxes, cigarette cases, ashtrays and desk sets.

Coral pictures can really bring out the creativity of the diver. Start with a piece of canvas board, which can be bought in any art supply store. Paint a background on the canvas with oil paints, watercolors, or acrylics. The background can be one solid color, or even an underwater scene. Or, the canvas can be covered with fabric, vinyl, or self-adhesive paper. The coral pieces are glued in place with epoxy glue or contact cement. After sufficient time for

A piece of staghorn coral is glued to an oil painted canvas to create a delicate coral picture.

drying, the picture can be hung with piano wire or adhesive picture hangers.

Tiny, fragile pieces of coral look well imbedded in plastic. Kits, including resin, a catalyst and molds, can be obtained at most hobby shops.

Specimens can also be displayed in a curio cabinet or on book shelves, either in decorative arrangements or separated by species and marked with identifying name tags, recording the type of coral, the date collected and the location of the find.

Another idea is to put together a natural setting in which

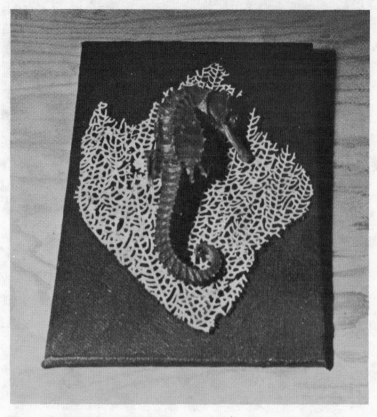

Above is a dried seahorse, mounted on a painted piece of dried sea fan. Both are glued to a painted canvas board for hanging.

to display the coral. A glass display case can be bought or built and the bottom spread with a light-colored sand. The branching coral, that must stand up to look natural, can be set in modeling clay bases. The bases can be camouflaged under mounds of sand. A few small shells and a starfish or two can be added to the scene.

Because of the abrasive nature of coral with the rough, protruding cups on its surface, it is difficult to dust. For cleaning unmounted pieces, simply dip them in fresh water, rinse and dry. Mounted pieces can be vacuumed or wiped with a soft damp cloth.

Coral specimen on display in a diver's home are intriguing souvenirs of his latest trip and are a great way of introducing non-diving friends to the beauties and complexities of the underwater world.

10 Cave Diving – Underwater Underground

A DIE-HARD OPEN water diver was heard asking, "Who would want to dive in a hole in the ground?" Well, apparently quite a number of divers would. Diving in water-filled holes—better known as cave diving—is becoming increasingly popular. Every year, for example, over 100,000 divers visit Florida springs and sinkholes alone.

What lures these adventurers into the inky chambers of subterranean caverns? Many of them began as dry cave explorers whose expeditions were frustrated by water-filled passages blocking the way. Others have come to the caves as former open water divers looking for yet another challenge.

One of the enticements to diving in the cave systems of springs is the unbelievable clarity of the water, usually offering visibility in excess of 100 feet. The crystal-clearness of the water combined with the spectacular settings of craigy cave entrances have lured many underwater photographers.

The relic hunter can look forward to finding arrowheads, old bottles and even bones of extinct animals in the deep recesses. In fact, archeology and fossil hunting are the most prevalent activities of cave divers.

The fish enthusiast will find unique fauna to study in this dark kingdom. Fish that swim upside down against the cave walls and blind, eye-less crustaceans await the cave diver with an interest in marine biology.

HOW CAVES ARE FORMED

Caves are underground chambers and passageways usually formed by the solvent action of water over a period of thousands of years. The freshwater caves visited by divers are primarily made of limestone which has been eroded by underground rivers.

A typical cave system in Florida may have its entrance at the bottom of a tiny lake nestled in the woods, as does Orange Sink, pictured below.

There are various types of cave systems. The freshwater cave diver can enjoy his sport in springs, sumps, sinks and syphons. Water is trapped under hydrostatic pressure, in a porous layer of earth called the aquifer. When this water breaks through the earth's crust it forms a spring. The spring resembles a small lake and water may flow into it through a cave system. A true spring always has an above-ground watercourse flowing away from it. This flow is called a run.

A syphon is the reverse phenomenon of a spring—the water flows back into the bowels of the earth instead of coming out of it. Syphons are extremely dangerous for diving since the swimmer must exit against the current.

A sink is a cavern formed by the collapsing of the surface crust or roof of an underground cave, which exposes the water within the cave. Unlike a spring, the sink never has a surface run and may therefore not be quite as clear.

A sump is a water-filled passage in a dry cave. The sump may continue for a few feet and then open onto a dry room or a partially air-filled chamber. On the other hand, it may continue totally filled with water for hundreds of feet.

Caves may also be found in the sea. These may be submerged all the time or only during high tides. Currents within sea caves are affected by the tides and the caves usually can be safely entered only at slack tide.

PIONEERS OF CAVE DIVING

The first cave diving expedition using scuba equipment was led by Captain Jacques Yves Cousteau, under the auspices of the French Office of Underseas Research. On August 27, 1946, Cousteau and Frederic Dumas became the first scuba divers to enter the famed Fountain of Vaucluse near Avignon, France.

Cousteau recalls in his book, The Silent World, his feelings as he lowered himself into the darkness of his first cave dive. "I glanced back and saw Didi (Dumas) gliding through the door against a faint green haze," he wrote. "The sky was no longer our business. We belonged now to a world where no light had ever struck."

The two pioneers penetrated 400 feet into the cave to a depth of approximately 200 feet. The first cave dive in his-

Upon entering a cave, the diver moves into a world of darkness, illuminated only by his light and that of his buddy.

tory almost had a disastrous end, because poisonous carbon-monoxide gas had inadvertently gotten into the tanks and nearly rendered the divers helpless as the noxious effects of the gas increased under pressure.

It took six years for cave diving to come to the United States. When it did, it made its debut out West. In 1953, the Western Speleological Institute organized a cave diving expedition. On this trip, Jon Lindbergh, a 20-year-old marine biology student and the son of the famous aviator Charles Lindberg, discovered and explored the Bower Cave in California, one of the largest underwater caverns in the western states.

In the same year, William Brown and Edward Simmons, members of the Southern California Chapter of the National Speleological Society, decided to probe the depths of Devil's Hole in Nevada to learn the secret of this hot spring's source. The two men organized a team and led them through several weeks of intensive practice sessions in obliging neighbors' pools and off local beaches. Underwater, they practiced emptying half-filled masks, reinserting the mouthpiece, adjusting air controls and buddy-breathing.

Finally, on August 1, 1953, Bill Brown donned a set of double tanks and lowered himself into the 93-degree water. On his first dive, he reached the 150-foot mark. His strong underwater lights penetrated the darkness for another 200 feet, yet the bottom was nowhere in sight. The group made many more dives during the following week, but the source of the spring was not discovered—nor has it been found to this day.

In the early days of cave diving, men went down alone and with makeshift equipment. Many of them didn't come back. Today, cave divers use perfected gear, the buddy system and safe techniques in an attempt to insure that the cavers will come back to log their dive.

THE DANGERS OF CAVE DIVING

Cave diving is not for the novice. Even an experienced open water diver needs special training, since diving in caves is different from any other type of scuba diving. The only activity remotely similar is ice diving.

The dangers of water-filled caves are myriad. First, and most importantly, the cave diver cannot make a direct free ascent to the surface in case of an emergency. Often, he must wind his way through hundreds of feet of passageways before he can ascend. This makes the problems of equipment malfunction or running out of air doubly serious.

Darkness is another hazard. Without light, the diver could wander in the complex maze of tunnels and never find his way out. Even if he has a light, the silt may reduce his visibility to zero.

Don't despair, however, because all of these dangers can

be overcome. Cave diving can be an enjoyable and relatively safe hobby with proper training, sufficient preparation and adequate equipment.

TRAINING FOR CAVE DIVING

As Jim Storey, cave diving expert of the National Speleological Society, so aptly put it, "Whatever the reason for cave diving, if you must try this madness, then be willing to prepare yourself for the worst of situations by becoming an expert diver."

Naturally, before a person can be a good cave diver, he must be a good diver, therefore the best way to start is by enrolling in a certified skin and scuba diving course. This will provide a good foundation on which to build cave diving skills.

After completing the course, the diver should strive to become proficient in the use of his equipment and confident of his abilities underwater. To obtain this he should accumulate at least 20 hours of open water diving time before he ventures into a cave.

When entering long mine shafts in quarries, divers should follow cave diving procedures. These tunnels can be hundreds of feet long and may branch off into several passageways.

The two most alien factors he will have to cope with on cave dives are darkness and close quarters. His practice must, therefore, include getting used to these two situations. To adapt to the darkness, the diver should make a number of open water night dives, mastering the use of lights and becoming familiar with operating in visibility limited to the range of his beam.

Saltwater coral caves are ideal places to get used to the confined feeling he will experience in caves. Coral caves—different than sea caves—are usually quite short. Most often daylight can be seen illuminating the exit.

The prospective cave diver should also do some practicing on land. He should know what a cave looks like, before venturing into a water-filled one. Visiting dry caves and observing the shape of the walls, the passageways which lead off from main rooms, and the general configuration, will make him better prepared for his first cave dive. Even a visit to a commercial cave, with all of its alternations and artificial lighting can be informative.

Back in the water, the diver should practice laying line with a reel and adjusting his buoyancy at various depths. He should learn how to breathe from a tank without a regulator and attempt to increase his breathholding ability by swimming underwater lengths in a pool in skin gear.

The diver should simulate emergency situations and, in open water, go through the motions of reacting to and solving them. These simulations should include running out of air, losing a member of the team, having all lights fail, getting tangled in the line, breaking the safety line, and subduing and saving a panicky buddy.

Once he feels confident enough to attempt a cave, the diver should begin in simple ones with easy access and exit and very few passageways branching off from the main rooms. On his first dives, he should not go in very far. Many popular caves even have signs posted underwater warning the novice cave diver not to proceed beyond that point. He should definitely heed that warning until he has the "feel" of caves and can be considered a veteran.

EQUIPMENT

The inside of a cave is no place to experience equipment malfunction, therefore, as important as it is to have the proper equipment for cave diving, it is even more important to maintain that equipment meticulously.

After a dive, all equipment should be rinsed in clean water and dried in an area out of the direct sunlight. Rubber wear should be inspected for rips and tears, regulators should never be stored without a dust cap over the high-pressure opening, and tanks should not be stored with less than 200 psi of air in them. Regulators should be taken to the dive shop for a yearly visual inspection check, and depth and pressure gauges should be tested periodically for accuracy.

Well-maintained open water diving equipment is, however, not sufficient for the cave diver, since he has problems no other diver encounters. But, since very little equipment is manufactured with the cave diver specifically in mind, he has had to alter and add to much of his gear—and even design some pieces from scratch.

The regulator is the single most important item since it feeds the life-sustaining air at a breathable pressure to the diver. An old regulator or a cheap model is not reliable enough for cave diving. The diver should buy the most dependable unit he can afford. It should be one which delivers large volumns of air, even at great depths, and should be easy breathing. A regulator with a balanced first stage and a downstream valve on the second stage delivers the most air with the least amount of effort.

A single hose regulator is preferable for cave diving over a double hose, since the hoses on a two-hose model are very flimsy and could easily be cut by the sharp rocks. Buddy-breathing is also more difficult with a two-hose regulator, particularly in a narrow passageway where it is impossible for the two divers to swim next to each other.

An absolutely vital accessory attached to the regulator is a *submersible pressure gauge*. It gives a constant reading of the amount of air remaining in the tank. Diving without one would be like taking off in an airplane without a gas gauge.

Depth, temperature of the water, and nervousness and physical condition of the diver all vary the rate at which he will use his air. The same diver may even consume different amounts of air on two identical dives, therefore without a pressure gauge, he could only guess at how much air is left.

The type and number of *tanks* used depend on the depth and duration of the planned dive. Anything smaller than a 71.2 cu. ft. tank is useful only for swimming through a short sump from one dry room to another.

Even the single 71.2 cu. ft. tank should only be worn on a short, simple cave dive. Most serious cave divers wear a pair of doubles—two 71.2 cu. ft. tanks connected by a twin tank valve assembly or a twin tank bar yoke.

The reserve or "J" valve used by the open water diver is useless to the caver. The small volume of air in a reserve is sufficient for getting to the surface—but hardly enough for swimming the long distance through passageways to the cave entrance and then up. Even if the diver was close enough to the entrance that the 300-pound reserve would seem to give him sufficient air, he might find he had breathed past it. The setup of the "J" valve makes it far too easy to trip the lever by bumping it against a wall. If the diver does not realize that it has been tripped until he needs the reserve, it is too late.

Because of these hazards, cave divers either use "K" or non-reserve valves or they place their "J" valves in the open position at the beginning of the dive and rely on a submersible pressure gauge.

There are two types of *emergency air systems* that can be used by the cave diver. One consists of an extra second stage and mouthpiece attached to a high pressure port of the regulator. This is primarily used for providing air to a buddy in trouble. It is far easier to offer a panicky diver his own mouthpiece than to try to get yours back from him.

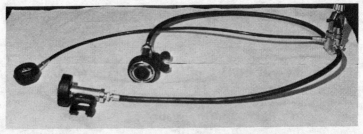

The octopus unit consists of two second-stages with mouthpieces. They are attached to the high-pressure port at the first stage of the regulator. The unit above also has a submersible pressure gauge.

A safety line is a vital piece of equipment. Here a diver is reeling in the line as he leaves the cave system. At right, the exhaust bubbles, exhaled by his team while they were in the cave below, filter through the crevices in the limestone.

This back-up second stage can also serve the diver if his main unit malfunctions during a dive.

The second type of emergency air system is a pony bottle fitted with a separate regulator. A pony bottle is an extra tank used only in case of emergency. It is attached to a set of twin tanks or to a single 71.2 cu. ft. tank. It may range in size from another full size tank to one holding only 5 to 10 cu. ft. of air. Some of them are attached to the other tanks in such a way that they can be removed underwater. Then the diver can give the whole rig—extra tank and regulator—to the buddy in trouble. This is particularly useful when the divers must swim in single file due to cramped quarters.

Following close behind the regulator in importance is the *safety line*. Cave systems wind and twist, branching out into many small passageways. The diver could easily take the wrong turn and get hopelessly lost. So, like Hansel and Gretel, he must leave a trail that he can follow back home. Instead of bread crumbs, the cave diver uses a line.

A strong line of 1/8" nylon is standard. Fishing line or monofilament should never be used as it is more tenacious than a spider's web. About 500 feet of line should be wound on a reel. Loose line quickly becomes unmanageable as it tangles, and is almost impossible to gather up after a dive. The reel should be equipped with a line guide to keep it from unreeling too fast and snarling.

The cave diver enters a world of darkness and so another of his primary pieces of equipment is a *light*. The diver should carry two underwater lights—one as his primary light source and the other as a backup. The primary light should be very strong and dependable with as high a candlepower as is available. Divers have used nickel-cadmium batteries or motorcycle batteries to devise their own homemade lights.

For maximum efficiency, one diver of the buddy pair may want to use a spotlight bulb for maximum penetration, while the other diver uses a floodlight bulb to light a wide area.

The second backup light may be smaller and less powerful, but it must be tested to be certain that it will operate under high pressure. A metal multi-cell flashlight which uses D cell batteries is good as a backup light.

Most cave divers wear *wet suits*. The obvious reason for wearing a wet suit is protection against the cold. Caves, other than those connected to hot springs, have water temperatures between sixty and seventy-eight degrees.

In addition to thermal protection, the suit provides protection from cuts, scrapes and abrasions caused by rocks and other sharp protrusions. Some divers even wear hoods to protect their heads from bumps as they duck under low ceilings.

The neoprene of the suit also provides additional buoyancy which will help the diver stay off the bottom. This is important to avoid kicking up clouds of silt and destroying visibility.

Sometimes the buoyancy in the suit is not enough to keep the diver from dragging on the bottom. In that case, a *flotation device* is needed. An ordinary inflatable life vest is not really efficient for this purpose. Besides being awkward to inflate orally in a cave, the vest raises the chest of the diver and still lets his feet drag.

Above are five examples of life vests which can be used as flotation devices by the cave diver. Since the one in the center has an auxiliary air supply, it offers an added margin of safety.

A one or two gallon plastic bottle is the simplest, cheapest and best flotation device. It can be filled with exhaust air from the regulator when buoyancy is needed and dumped out as the diver becomes too buoyant.

There are now on the market special buoyancy cylinders which can be attached to the tank. These are quite efficient, but a good bit more expensive than a plastic bottle.

A *depth gauge* and a reliable *diving watch* are both important for calculating decompression. A cave can be very deceptive about depth. When the floor and the ceiling of a passageway remains the same distance apart, the diver may think he is staying at the same depth, while, in fact, he may be descending rapidly.

Since cave diving is multi-level diving with the depths varying considerably during a single dive, an *automatic decompression meter* is a valuable instrument to have. The cave diver may spend only a minute at the deepest point of his dive yet without a decompression meter, he would have to calculate his dive as if he had been at the deepest point for the entire dive. The decompression meter takes into account the changes in depth during a dive and thus extends the wearer's time underwater within the no-decompression limits, or shortens his decompression stops.

A *knife* should be carried in a sheath strapped to the calf or thigh. In case a diver gets tangled inextricably in the line, the knife can be used as a last resort.

A plastic slate with a graphite pencil is handy for underwater communications. A grease pencil can also be carried. It will write on most anything—the diver's hand, a wet suit, a rock.

Inflatable boats have greatly assisted cave divers. They can be used to carry the diver and his equipment across a large spring to the point of descent, thereby conserving the diver's energy and air. A boat such as the one manufactured by Zodiac can be assembled and pumped up at the dive site in twenty minutes, and yet be carried in the trunk of a car.

PLANNING THE DIVE

The first thing to do when planning a cave dive is to find out everything possible about the cave in which the dive

An inflatable boat is very handy when water must be crossed to reach a cave entrance or the cavers must travel through half-filled caverns to reach the dive spot. This Zodiac folds compactly enough to be carried by the divers to any area. Then it can be inflated, using a simple foot pump, in less than twenty minutes.

will take place. The most important things to learn are the depth of the cave, the size of the passageways, what normal visibility is and what the silting conditions are—if there are any currents, if there are permanent guidelines in the cave, and if maps of the cave system are available. The local dive shop is the best place to look for this data. If the dive shop owner is unable to supply the information, he usually knows from whom it can be obtained.

Since every expedition needs a leader, a Divemaster should be selected. His job is to set the ground rules of the dive, establish signals, and lead the group into the cave. It is best to choose the most experienced cave diver in the group for this important position.

Even though several divers may be going into the cave single file on one line, the Divemaster should see to it that they each have a buddy. It is far easier to keep track of one buddy than to try to keep an eye on everyone in the team.

It is a good idea for divers to get used to working with one particular buddy. In time, a buddy pair will get to know each other so well that they can anticipate each other's actions. This closeness can be vital in an emergency in a cave.

Before the dive, the Divemaster sets depth and time limitations. This limitation should be adhered to if at all possible, and altered only if the unexpected happens. The maxim "plan your dive and dive your plan" is especially applicable to cave diving.

Based on the plan, air consumption must be calculated and plenty of extra air allowed. The entire dive plan should be made with the *weakest* member of the team in mind. By the same token, air consumption figuring should consider the abilities of the person who normally uses the most air on a dive.

Ideally, a backup surface team should be on shore during the dive, with their equipment ready so that they could go down immediately in the event of an emergency. If this is not possible, the divers should at least inform someone on shore that they will be cave diving, what cave they will be in and when they expect to be back. After the dive, they should check with this person. If they do not, he must sound an alarm and begin a search.

At a final briefing session before the dive, the Divemaster goes over the dive plan and sets up communications signals. The standard hand signals are usually used, but in case darkness or silt obscures the hand signals, signals using lights or noise, such as tapping on the tank, must be established.

Just before each diver takes the plunge, he should thoroughly check his equipment paying special attention to his air supply, lights and lines.

When everyone is ready, the Divemaster ties the safety line to a stationary object on shore—such as a tree—and leads the group down to the opening of the cave.

IN THE CAVE

In case someone tampers with the line on shore, the Divemaster should secure the line a second time, just inside the entrance to the cave. A simple way to do this is to make a loop, put it around a prominent rock and secure it with a clothespin. The clothespin is far easier to remove on the way out than a knot would be.

Since the Divemaster is first, he is the reel man and must lay the guideline. He must be careful to reel the line out slowly and keep it taut. It is the job of the second diver to position the line so that it won't snag or be cut by sharp projections.

All the other divers hold the line, using it as a guide—not as a means of pulling themselves into the cave. The easiest way to grasp the line is to make an "O" with all four fingers and thumb and slide the line through this circle.

The line should be kept at arm's length and to one side of the diver to avoid becoming entangled in it. If he swims under the line, he may snag his tank valve, and if he swims over it, he will be kicking it with his fins.

Permanent lines are sometimes installed in popular cave systems. They usually begin several hundred feet into the cave so that novice divers will not use them and swimmers will not tamper with them. If there are permanent lines, the reel man uses his line from the surface, into the cave and up to these lines. He then ties off his line, leaves the reel and proceeds on the permanent line. All other divers proceed exactly as if they were on a temporary safety line.

The divers should swim as close to the ceiling as

possible, to avoid kicking up the millions of little particles of silt covering the bottom. As previously mentioned, if the diver is negatively buoyant, buoyancy devices can help him stay off the bottom.

When swimming in a cave the diver should use a very gentle kick. If the ceiling is low and the silt thick, he may want to use the technique of "finger-walking." As the name suggests, the diver does not kick at all, but pulls himself along the bottom by walking on his fingers.

When a strong current rushes out of the cave, the diver may have to pull himself in by holding onto rocks jutting out from the sides of the cave. A current like this is a bonus on the return swim, because the tired diver can ride out with the current, often without swimming a stroke.

In syphon diving, when the current flows into the cave, the diver must be cautious before he enters. It will be very easy to get in, but he might find it *impossible* to swim out against the strong current.

In an emergency situation, in a cave more than anywhere else, the basic rule is *stay calm*. Nothing is worse than a panicky diver, and his mindless actions can take a whole team to their death with him.

Therefore, if a dangerous situation occurs, or even approaches, the Divemaster should give the prearranged signal and abort the dive. All divers then acknowledge the signal and leave the cave in an orderly manner.

If a member of the team runs out of air or his equipment malfunctions, he first calmly gives his buddy the no-air sign (moving his forefinger across his throat in a cutting motion). They then begin buddy breathing and one of them gives the abort signal to a third member of the team who passes it on. The entire team then starts out, keeping an eye on the diver in trouble.

Another emergency is a lost diver. If the diver stays on the line he won't get lost, but in case he does he should swim up near the ceiling, breathe shallowly and wait in one spot. If he swims around to look for the team, he may only be going farther and farther away. Once he is in position, he should wave his light back and forth in a 360 degree circle and periodically tap on his tank.

As soon as his buddy realizes that he is missing, he will signal the rest of the group. Then each member of the team should carefully rotate his light in all directions to search for the missing diver. They should check the floor of the cave in case he has passed out.

If this doesn't work, then the Divemaster signals all divers to hang on to the line and turn out their lights. In the silent darkness, everyone looks for the gleam of the lost diver's light and listens for the sound of tapping.

If he still isn't found, the line should be tied off and the reel left, while the group backtracks and looks for him. Never, never take the line up with a lost diver still in the cave, because it is his last chance of finding his way out if he is not located by his diving team. The line would also be a guide for a search and rescue mission.

A lost diver can cost one life, but sudden, total silting can be surprising and dangerous to the whole team. When this happens, all divers should stop immediately, hold securely to the line and wait for the silt to clear. If there is a current in the cave, it will carry the silt away. If it doesn't, the reel man secures the line, leaves the reel, and moves back on the line until he is in hand contact with his buddy. They continue backing up until each man's hand touches the one next to him on the line. Then, with each diver having only one hand on the line, the Divemaster counts the hands by touch. If all are present, they slowly and carefully leave the cave, never letting go of the line.

If a diver becomes tangled in the line during a dive, he should signal his buddy to untangle him—not cut the rope. Before resorting to cutting the rope, the diver should remove his equipment—keeping his regulator in his mouth—and untangle the gear.

The Divemaster should be certain to turn around well before anyone's tank drops to the half-full mark. He must remember that tired divers may use up more air on the way out than they did going in. When leaving the cave, the reel man is the last diver out, reeling the line in as he goes. This job will slow him down and his buddy should stick with him, helping him to keep the line taut for tangle-free reeling.

One special technique for diving in sumps must be mentioned. When the diver surfaces into a dry room that has never before been explored, he should continue to breathe

When leaving the cave, the reelman is the last one out, reeling in the line as he goes.
Here, he leaves the gloom of the cave to follow his teammates out into the sunshine.

from his regulator until he tests the air. Divers have died
from breathing foul, poisonous air in newly discovered
chambers.

DECOMPRESSION

Cave diving brings up several unusual decompression
problems. The Navy dive tables are based on a diver going
down to one depth, staying at that level and then ascending
vertically to the surface. Cave diving rarely, if ever, is like
that. The diver may enter the cave system at 65 feet, swim
up to 25, down to 60 and then make a sharp drop to 150. Because of this variation, an Automatic Decompression
Meter is very handy since it takes into account the actual
depths at which the diver was swimming.

Another decompression problem occurs because the
normal ascent rate of 60 feet per minute is difficult, if not
impossible, to maintain in a cave. The last sixty feet of
ascent may consist of a diagonal swim of 250 feet and may
take as much as five minutes. Or the diver may even have

(Photo by D. Edward May)

The author checks her camera equipment before entering the cave system at the bottom of this spring. To photograph the inky recesses, she uses a Nikonos with a flash attachment.

to swim back down before he can continue up. Here again, a Decompression Meter comes in handy.

If decompression is planned, a spare SCUBA rig for each diver is normally placed at the first decompression stop. The air should be turned off to prevent leakage. Although there are ways of figuring this type of decompression without a meter, the novice cave diver should abide by the no decompression tables. (See chapter one.)

DEBRIEFING

After the dive, a debriefing session is held during which the Divemaster checks to make sure that everyone returned and that they are all in good condition. The group should review their goals and what they accomplished. They should discuss the adequacy of their equipment and how they can improve equipment or techniques in the future. The dive should be logged, noting time, depth, air consumption, discoveries, etc.

WHERE TO CAVE DIVE

Florida is the number one state for the cave diver, with the best areas in the northern part of the state on the Suwannee and Santa Fe Rivers. In that area, Dale Stone of Branford, Florida, who runs the Aqua Shack, can recommend local diving spots—plus the safe procedures of cave diving.

Missouri ranks next in the number of cave diving locations. There are also exciting caves to be explored in Tennessee, Alabama, California, Nevada, Georgia, Kentucky, Oklahoma, Texas and Virginia.

11 Careers in Diving

THE SPORT DIVER who develops a true love of scuba diving may come to find that he wants to spend more than just his few leisure hours in the underwater world. For him or her, a career in diving might be just the answer.

Oceanography is a field with a growth potential greater than any other area. At the beginning of World War II, there were fewer than 50 oceanographers in the United States. Today, over 5,000 claim that title and many, many more work in and with the sea under various other titles and job descriptions.

There is room in the sea for every type of person from the scientist with a Ph.D to the laborer who never finished elementary school. Anyone with an urge to earn his living from the sea, should first look to his other interests and talents. Most skills can be applied to underwater work and, if he first chooses an area in which he excels or is at least interested, he will have a better chance at success.

PASSING ON THE KNOWLEDGE

A diver who truly enjoys the sport will want to share his pastime with others and introduce them to his underwater world. If he has a knack for teaching, he can turn this desire into a diving career. Thousands of people are learning to dive every year and the need for good, qualified instructors is growing.

To make sure that his course will meet the highest standards and that the certification he gives to his students will be nationally recognized, the diver must become a certified instructor. The three top organizations for certifying instructors are the YMCA, NAUI (National Association of Underwater Instructors) and PADI (Professional Association of Diving Instructors).

Each one of these associations holds qualifying institutes for prospective instructors, and also sets mandatory guidelines for the course an instructor gives. The tests at these institutes include swimming ability, skin and scuba skills, written examinations and extemporaneous speaking. For more information on the requirements and the location and dates of the institutes, the diver can write to:

YMCA NATIONAL SCUBA HEADQUARTERS
1611 Candler Building
Atlanta, Ga. 30303

NAUI HEADQUARTERS
22809 Barton Road
Grand Terrace (Colton), Ca. 92324

PROFESSIONAL ASSOCIATION OF DIVING
INSTRUCTORS
P.O. Box 177
Costa Mesa, California

If making a career of teaching, it is often a good idea to become certified by more than one association. This gives the instructor a little more flexibility, and he would be able to offer whatever certification a student requests.

Once a diver is a certified instructor, there are several avenues open to him. He could teach in his own city at one or more of the local YMCA or neighborhood pools. This would normally be a part-time job, since most courses are given in the evenings, once or twice a week.

To turn his teaching into a full-time job, he could contact a nearby high school or college and convince them to add scuba diving as a physical education elective. Or, if he lives in a large city, he may want to make arrangements with a popular hotel to use their pool for his classes. Then, he might be able to act as their recreation or pool director, thereby making the hours when he is not teaching scuba profitable.

Instruction can be the diver's entree into a life on the island or at the resort area of his dreams. In any oceanside location with a large draw for vacationers, instructors have set up diving schools with condensed but comprehensive courses for tourists, offering dive trips to their graduated students.

CHARTER CAPTAINS

This leads consequently to another occupation that often goes hand-in-hand with instruction in a resort area—the job of captain of a dive boat and guide on underwater excursions.

Like instructing, chartering can be a part-time occupation in a coastal town that is not a resort area, or it can be a full-time job at a location where tourists visit year-round.

Depending on his area, the charter captain could ferry divers to reefs or to shipwrecks and guide them through their dive so that they don't miss the highlights of the dive site. For this type of work, the captain would need a large boat with a minimum capacity of six to eight divers plus gear. He will have to have a captain's license, and should carry insurance. Requirements for charter boats vary with the area and should be checked before an operation is set up. The Coast Guard Station in the area is a good place to go for these regulations.

If his boat is also equipped with depth finders, sonar,

and Loran, the captain will have a better chance of finding the best dive spots. His reputation will grow and his trips will be booked well in advance. Of course, anyone running charters must become thoroughly familiar with his area so that he can take his customers to whatever kind of local dive spot they request.

Rates range from $5.00 per diver for a half-day trip to as much as $30.00 or more for a full day trip with food provided. Rates vary with the popularity of the locale, the size of the group, and the distance to the dive site. In resort areas, prices may also change seasonally. It is wise for the charter captain to take bookings in advance and ask for deposits, so that he does not lose a day's profits when a group fails to show up.

In resort areas, the charter captain will often work through one of the major hotels. Sometimes, he may even have a dive shop on the premises. Whether he has a shop or not, he should keep a sizable inventory of diving gear for customers who don't bring their equipment with them.

Charter Captain, Charlie Stratton, operates the dive boat, *Bottom Time,* **out of Manasquan Inlet in Brielle, N.J. He ferries divers to the many shipwrecks off the Jersey shore.**

It is especially important to have tanks and weight belts since many divers would rather rent these than pay high overweight luggage charges on an airline.

DIVE SHOP OWNER

Anywhere there are divers, there is a need for a good, reputable dive shop. Successful dive shop operations are not limited to the coasts. The Midwest is a lucrative area because of all the Great Lakes and quarry divers. But, even states considered arid, like Arizona and Nevada, have thriving diving equipment businesses.

(Official U.S. Navy Photograph)

Al Catalfumo, owner of Diver's Cove in Lawrence Harbor, N.J., knows the importance of providing good air fills. He uses a bank of cylinders which he fills from his own compressor. When tanks are being filled, he immerses them in cool water in the square metal container so that the diver gets a full, cold fill.

In addition to selling equipment, the shop owner should sell good, clean air fills. Local divers will be in the shop every week for air, and this will lead to sales of equipment.

When setting up a shop, the prospective owner must contact diving equipment manufacturers to establish credit and obtain an initial inventory. Sometimes an exclusive will be available in his area. The dive shop should be in an accessible location and should have a diver's flag prominently displayed.

Although owning a dive shop is not an occupation which allows the owner to work underwater, it is a good base from which to operate other pursuits. The first place a diver will ask about charters is his local dive shop, so often the shop owner will also be a charter captain. Many owners are scuba instructors and draw students the same way. Also, a dive shop owner could organize and guide diving vacations several times a year.

JOIN THE NAVY AND SEE THE UNDERWATER WORLD

The first picture that comes to mind when discussing careers in diving is usually one of the Navy Frogman, swimming silently through dark water to a hostile beach.

These divers are called UDT Men or members of the U.S. Navy Underwater Demolition Team. They have long been the symbol of the champions among the diving community, since their standards and qualifications are very high, the training is rigorous, and the entire corps is volunteer. Since they are classified as combat troops, the program, at the time of this writing, is not open to women.

To apply for the Team, a man must first meet normal Navy enlistment standards, must be a citizen of the United States, and be between the ages of 18 and 31. If he is already in the Navy, he must have at least 24 months of obligated service left when he graduates from the training, or be willing to extend his enlistment for that period of time.

The applicant must be able to swim 300 yards in seven minutes, run a mile in seven and a half minutes, and do at least six continuous pullups and 30 continuous sit-ups. He may have 20/30 bilateral vision if it is correctable to 20/20. He must achieve a score of at least 50 on the General

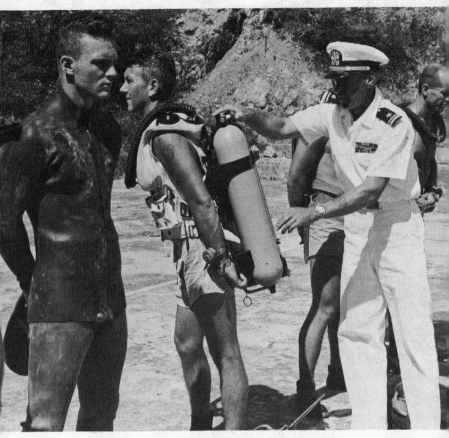

(Official U. S. Navy Photograph)

A UDT officer inspects the equipment of a trainee before he goes into the water for a training exercise.

Classification Test and pass physical qualification exams for duty involving diving.

When the entrance tests have been passed, the work begins. There is a rigorous 24-week course, which has a high drop-out rate. The training begins at either the East Coast or West Coast UDT Base.

The first 16 weeks are devoted to physical conditioning. Calisthenics, endurance swims, obstacle course, drills, life-saving techniques, and forced marches are all part of this phase of training. Chart reading, photo interpretation, communications, intelligence, first aid and other mental skills are also learned and practiced. The final exam is a seven-mile open water swim.

The group then moves on to qualify as parachutists and finally comes to the Underwater Swimmers School. There they learn the principles and use of SCUBA, underwater navigation, harbor searches, and locking in and out of submarines. After graduation from the training, each man is on probation for six months before he becomes a full-fledged member of the UDT.

In wartime, the UDT man is a demolition expert who is part commando. He is first man on the beach, and usually moves in, accomplishes his mission, and moves out—all undetected. In peacetime, this group is entrusted with various vital aquatic tasks. For example, it is members of the UDT who recover the capsules carrying America's returning astronauts.

In wartime, UDT men are often dropped off to accomplish their mission and picked up later via the stringline recovery method, pictured below.

Any civilian interested in this exciting life should contact his local Navy Recruiter for information on the UDT Pre-Enlistment Program.

DIVING SCIENTISTS

There is room in the ocean for most any type of scientist. Although some diving scientists do have degrees in oceanography, most of them do not. Their educational background can be in any number of various scientific fields, and they adapt this knowledge to underwater work.

The chemist can study the chemical makeup of sea water. He will don his diving gear to collect water specimen from various depths, temperature ranges and areas to bring back to his laboratory for analysis and comparison.

The marine geologist is interested in the ocean floor. He will dive to bring up sediment and bottom samples from the surface of the sea bottom, and also dig down into the sand and silt to obtain core samples.

One of the most fascinating sciences of the underwater world is marine biology, the study of life within the sea, ranging from microscopic plankton to the gigantic whales, and including also marine plant life. When the study is limited to the fishes, it is called ichthyology.

One of the most famous diving ichthyologists is Dr. Eugenia Clark. Her work has taken her diving around the world from Micronesia to the island to Ngulu. She is best known for her study of sharks and for helping to found the Cape Haze Marine Laboratory in Sarasota, Florida.

Another science readily adaptable to the sea is archeology. Underwater archeology is basically treasure hunting with serious, scientific purposes and methods added. Commander Mendel Peterson, the Director of Underwater Projects for the Smithsonian Institute, has dived on Spanish galleons, sunken cities, and other archeological sites to record history underwater.

Diving scientists can find work in private industry, at museums, for foundations, at marine laboratories, and as civilian government employees. In preparation for this type of work, college training should include some courses in oceanography and the marine sciences, even if the

Commander Mendel Peterson, an underwater archeologist, prepares to don a hookah outfit and visit a 17th century shipwreck in the Bermuda waters below.

science degree will be in some other specialty. For a list of colleges in the U.S. which offer courses in oceanography, write to The Committee on Research, Education, and Facilities, Building 159E, Room 476, Navy Yard, Washington, D.C. 20390, and ask for the pamphlet on University Curricula in Oceanography. In addition to a listing of colleges, this brochure gives an outline of typical four-year courses of study.

THE TECHNICIAN

A technician is basically the backup man for the scientist. Once the scientist has set up a research pattern, it may fall to the technician to carry it out—collecting bottom samples, gathering marine specimens, making underwater sketches, maps and drawings, or doing manual work like soldering, cutting or setting traps.

This type of diver has scientific knowledge and tendencies but prefers to work with his hands. Two years of post-high school training at a junior college or technical school is needed to qualify for most technician positions.

The range of job opportunities for the technician is about the same as for a scientist, since most industries and organizations which hire scientist need technicians, also.

To train as a technician, one might look to the junior colleges which offer associate certificates in oceanographic technology. Peninsula College at Port Angeles, Washington, for example, has a program to train technicians in fish handling and hatchery operations. Southern Maine Vocational Technical Institute at South Portland teaches marine diesel engineering, marine laboratory assistance, seamanship and geological oceanography among other subjects.

SALVAGE, CONSTRUCTION AND REPAIR

Other divers who like to work with their hands can participate in the building, repairing and salvage of manmade materials in the underwater world.

The ocean is a great lost-and-found repository, making the work of the salvage diver very important. His assignments may range from retrieving a 20 horsepower motor from the bottom of a 30-foot lake, to attempting to raise the massive Andrea Dorea from her watery grave over 200 feet down in the cold North Atlantic.

Salvage divers should be able to use tools competently on land, and then learn to adapt these skills to underwater work. Working with tools underwater is very different from on land. For example, using an ordinary wrench, the diver would find himself turning, instead of the bolt.

A salvage diver can work with just one buddy, form a partnership of several divers, or go to work for a large established underwater salvage firm. Clients may range from marine insurance companies to private individuals. Bidding on government salvage contracts may also bring in lucrative business. The pay per hour for salvage diving is high, but the diver who is new in the business may find that in the beginning jobs are few and far between. As his reputation grows, however, his calendar will fill up.

For large salvage projects, the diver will need boats,

barges, cranes and other costly equipment. Unless his operation is large enough to own these items, he can usually rent them on a job-by-job basis.

Most salvage divers also do underwater repair work. This may include ship or yacht maintenance, repair of barriers and sea walls, working on buoys, and even inspecting and cleaning submerged pipelines and drainage systems.

In the oil industry, divers are needed to service well heads, inspect and repair off-shore rigs, and help in setting up drilling platforms.

(Official U.S. Navy Photograph)

Two salvage divers install explosive stud guns to the lift legs of the Large Object Salvage System. They work in 110 feet of water.

Scuba divers are now used for marine construction of all types. They may be called on to help in bridge or tunnel building. Construction divers of the future may even be building submarine cities like the complex planned off the Hawaiian Islands.

As with the salvage diver, the underwater construction worker can solicit his own contracts or can work for large established firms. The biggest company in this field is a world-wide organization called International Underwater Contractors. They have U.S. offices in New York City.

"TEST PILOT"

With all the new developments and inventions for use in the underwater world, someone is needed to test these products before they can go on the market. A diver may become the "test pilot" on a research and development team and test sport diving equipment or industrial instrumentation.

A particular area where "guinea pig" divers are most needed is in testing the powers of man to live beneath the sea. Underwater habitats have been set up to prove that man can live and work effectively underwater. Some of these already completed have been Jacques Cousteau's ConShelf experiments, the U.S. Navy's Sealab projects, Ed Link's SPID venture in the Bahamas, and the Tektite experiments.

In each of these ambitious undertakings, men lived in the habitat for days or weeks at a time and made daily excursions in scuba equipment around their underwater home. The divers who lived in Sealab II included a physician, a mechanical engineer, an aeronautical engineer, geologists, biologists, physical and military oceanographers. Plus, Scott Carpenter, one of the original astronauts, spent a few weeks in the habitat. As can be seen, divers from several occupations are needed for habitat experiments.

The sport diver who would like to spend some time in a habitat to see if that type of work would appeal to him, should go to the Bahamas on his next vacation. At the Underwater Explorers Club in Freeport there is a habitat that can be occupied by the amateur diver for two or three days at a time.

PHOTOGRAPHY

The field of underwater photography is relatively new, and talent is needed in all phases of the art. As mentioned in the chapter devoted to underwater photography, the diver should first develop his talents on land. Then, with experimentation and/or a course in underwater photography, he is ready to go commercial.

Underwater still photographs can be sold to magazines and newspapers. They may also be bought by advertising agencies for use in advertisements. The diving photographer should assemble a portfolio of his best work to show when applying for a job or an assignment.

Another phase of photography that is growing even faster is underwater movies. Photographers are needed to shoot short underwater sequences to be used in full-length feature films. Also, a market is developing for full-length underwater films. Television, particularly, looks for underwater specials and has even carried some series featuring underwater action. Shooting the underwater television commercial is also a very profitable occupation. One cameraman traveled to Spain to shoot a diver swimming for 30 seconds and then surfacing for a nice cold beer.

Photography is needed by scientists for recording geological, biological, archeological and chemical data. Industry, too, uses underwater photographers, as did A T & T. Divers went down in a Perry Cubmarine to make a photo survey of American Telephone and Telegraph's Transatlantic Cable. Several potential trouble spots were detected and repaired.

RESOURCES FROM THE SEA

The sea is rich in minerals, just waiting to be gathered. Diamonds, gold, tin and manganese have been mined by divers using dredges, air-lifts and other tools. Many divers have already made small fortunes working in pairs or teams gathering gold. Like the old 49ers, however, these divers take a big gamble.

But, established mining companies are now looking for efficient ways of retrieving the ocean's mineral wealth, and most of them employ divers.

The technology for the acquisition of the sea's oil is already highly developed. The birth of marine drilling occurred in the early 1930s when oil was first tapped from the Louisiana bayous in six feet of water. Today, more than 50 floating rigs dot the ocean, and drilling has been successful in hundreds of feet of water.

In 1967, two divers, Arthur Pachette and Glen Taylor, repaired an oil well head at a depth of 636 feet off the coast of Louisiana. They spent six days in a decompression chamber after that job.

Many divers are needed to work on the oil rigs. For this work, however, a diver must have a thorough and expert knowledge of the workings and repair of this complicated equipment. It is well worth the effort of learning, because the pay is high.

Besides the mineral resources, one of the greatest resources of the sea is food. There is more than 400 billion tons of organic material produced annually in the sea, without any cultivation by man. Man has, not yet even begun to use a fraction of that wealth.

Divers do dive for abalone, lobsters, oysters and clams, but only in very small quantities. In the future, there will be diving farmers—or aquaculturists—harvesting seaweed beds and gathering animal life into pens. Already some of this underwater farming is beginning, and grants are available from the government to establish businesses for cultivating and gathering food from the sea.

Divers have been helpful in the building and maintenance of artificial reefs. These reefs, made of old tires, auto bodies, and large appliances, promote fish life by providing homes for marine animals. Fish and lobster populations around artificial reefs have soared within one season.

SCUBA SHERIFFS AND DIVING DETECTIVES

Underwater law enforcement is an entirely new field. Here, the diver with a background in police work will find his niche. France's Mediterranean Coast already boasts a large underwater patrol to enforce skin and scuba diving regulations and to keep looters off of restricted shipwrecks.

An underwater police force can be far more effective than officers in a boat for detecting fish poaching. They can also guard against drug running and smuggling via water.

Divers are employed even by inland police departments for the unpleasant but necessary job of body recovery from lakes and rivers.

A diver can now work underwater as a State Park Ranger. The first underwater state park in the nation, John Penekamp Coral Reef State Park, has been established. Other underwater parks will most likely follow.

Underwater insurance investigators are needed to verify claims of accidental sinkings of yachts and commercial boats. The famous Italian detective, Tom Ponzi, who owns Mercurius Agency, employs several scuba divers, and is himself a diver. They have investigated pleasure boat wrecks and have also used diving for gathering information and for investigations.

OTHER OCCUPATIONS

Most any background on land can be applied to the sea.

Anyone who wants to work underwater can find a way to adapt his or her career.

A writer or journalist can join the staff of a diving magazine or oceanographic publication which will entail reporting on dive trips. Or he could work as a free-lance writer and sell the story of his diving adventures to magazines, book publishers and newspapers.

A lawyer might specialize in marine law and participate in research projects underwater. A salesman can take on a line of diving equipment. In the course of his work, he will have opportunities to demonstrate his wares.

An artist or a draftsman may find himself doing underwater sketching or mapping on an archeological dive site. A designer of museum exhibits was sent on many exciting dive trips to view the marine environment first-hand, so that she could recreate it in an exhibit.

Most students take diving lessons merely as a lark. Many of these, however, have found that it has turned into an infatuating avocation. For some, diving has even changed the direction of their careers. Like the siren that she is, the sea calls and the diver answers, going to play and to work in her depths.